#VANCHURCH

#VanChurch

Spiritual Lessons from Life on the Road

ANNA AND JIM HALL

Cane Mill Press

Copyright © 2022 by Anna and Jim Hall

All rights reserved. No part of this book may be reproduced in any manner whatsoever without written permission except in the case of brief quotations embodied in critical articles and reviews.

First Printing, 2022

Cane Mill Press

Scottdale, GA 30079

www.canemillpress.com

editor@canemillpress.com

Library of Congress Control Number: 2022915704

ISBN/SKU 978-1-7375604-4-9

EISBN 978-1-7375604-5-6

CONTENTS

About #VanChurch	1
1 Lesson One: Find Your Place	3
2 Lesson Two: Make a Map	7
3 Lesson Three: Cross Your Rubicon	23
4 Lesson Four: Be a Stranger in a Strange Land	40
5 Lesson Five: Find Your Center	50
6 Lesson Six: Brake for Delight	65
7 Lesson Seven: Lose Your Place	84
8 Lesson Eight: Stay Rooted and Keep Branching	98
9 Lesson Nine: Home by Another Road	110

| 10 | Lost and Found: A Postscript | 123 |

31 Days Of #VanChurch Devotions   127

Notes   159

ACKNOWLEDGEMENTS

Thanks to everyone who has supported us during our travels and travails. We love y'all.

About #VanChurch

Writing a book with another person is a strange exercise. Do you discuss every word? Divide and conquer? Muddle through however you can?

When we decided to write a book about our van adventures, we took the divide and conquer approach. Jim, with his historians eye, did the location and historical research to reinforce what we learned as we traveled. Anna wrote the narrative, so when you read "I" you are reading Anna's voice about their shared adventures, or Anna's philosophical and theological musings on those experiences. We worked together on how to structure the book. Jim selected the photos, and Anna did the layout and design. Hopefully, it makes sense, is a fun read, and inspires your own adventures on the road.

P.S. About our dogs: The first year, we only had Poppy. By the second year, we had added Pepper to the family. Since we chose a thematic approach rather than a chronological one, some stories mention our singular dog, while others mention dogs, plural. In case you feel at times like we have a disappearing dog, you can rest easy knowing they are both still here as of 2022 and enjoying long days of hikes, treats, meals, and frequent barking at all delivery people. They also can't wait for our next van adventure!

Poppy and Pepper, Back Porch at Home

| 1 |

Lesson One: Find Your Place

What is your latitude and longitude right now?
What is your exact street location?
Where does the water flow when rain falls where you are?
Who else lived where you are in years past?
What ecosystem are you in?
What type of land lies under your feet or under the building you are in right now? Is it a plain, a ridge, a mountain range?

There are infinite ways we can describe our physical location at any given time. We may be explaining our life situation, making small talk, giving someone directions to find us, or simply orienting ourselves. "Plug this address into your navigation system," we say, or "Go past where the old store used to be, down to the big old barn, turn left there, and we are the third house on the right."

We also describe where we are in other ways.
Where are you in your career?
How old are you?
Are you married?
What degree do you have?

These locations in life help people put us in categories or know how to start a conversation with us. They also help us know where we might want to go from here, on our next trip, or on our larger life journey.

To get anywhere, we first have to know where we are. So when me and my husband and dogs took the first tiny steps toward traveling all over the country in a van, where exactly were we?

We were, in a sense, bogged down.

In December of every year, I make an inventory of sorts. I make lists of what we can celebrate from the past 12 months, and what we are happy to leave behind. I begin dreaming and visioning what I hope the months ahead will hold. At the end of 2017, when it was time for this exercise, I realized that I felt stuck. It seemed that for the first time since our marriage, no goal or objective was pulling us forward. We had a house, two good jobs, and had finished our educations. What else was there to work toward? At the same time, being in mid-life felt like we were running out of road.

We had recently ended our long journey of trying to become parents. This journey took us through fertility treatments, losing our daughter, Millie, shortly after birth, and failing in our efforts to adopt through foster care and private adoption. A confusing and random set of circumstances stopped that quest. We didn't make the decision to stop as much as the decision was made for us by life situations. We ran out of money for private adoption before being chosen by any birth mothers. Then, a storm took down a tree, leaving us without electricity for a week. Of course, that was the week we received a call for our first possible foster care placement. The social worker on the phone described a placement for an older child, not the baby or toddler our tiny house had been approved and prepared for, a true challenge even if our house had power. Without electricity, we had to say no. Our older dog began having some behavioral issues, probably due to all the house chaos. From that point on, we only received calls for short-term respite (read: babysitting), often when we were out of town and not there to help.

After seeing a brother and sister go out the door screaming and crying that they didn't want to be moving from one foster family to another, we realized something crucial: our grief over Millie was still not at the point we could be fully present for those in the midst of such grief themselves.

The day when we told them to put our home on hold was an anticlimax, albeit one full of tears and self-examination. We never made a formal or final decision to stop our journey toward parenthood. But with both of us well past 40, we realized we might be entering a future we hadn't truly considered since early in our marriage -- two adults, no kids, a dog or two.

This realization (or resignation) took the wind out of our sails. What was next? We had finished our education, with multiple terminal and professional degrees between us. Our work lives, mostly satisfying, didn't hold the possibility of advancement milestones or higher positions to work toward.

It seemed we were empty nesters without ever having a nest. But we didn't know anyone our age living like that. Without an example among our friends and family, we couldn't envision our future life in a way that made us eager to begin it.

2017 was also the year of The Health Issue, mysterious pain for 11 months which turned out to be as simple to resolve as a single outpatient procedure. During the many months of doctors not being able to figure things out, it felt like we had entered a future we very much did not want of endless medical visits punctuating periods of inactivity and much anxiety due to low grade pain. Food contributed to the problem, so our previous date nights of dinners out and exotic fare from the international neighborhoods near our home were put on hold. We worked, we watched TV, we slept. The only road we traveled was our street where we walked the dogs 1000 times, up and down, in front of our house.

One morning, not too long after my medical procedure restored my health in November 2017, I woke up with an idea -- we should get a camper van.

It was not a new idea to me. In truth, I began researching camper vans on my first home computer in my early 20s. Before YouTube or

Google, back in the late 1990s, I visited message boards full of pictures and conversations about Volkswagen Westphalias and Eurovans and dreamed about hitting the road. While the online platforms changed over the years, as did the approaches to what became known as #vanlife, my longing for this type of adventure ebbed and flowed but never completely left me.

In this new age of #vanlife influencers posting Instagram stories, YouTube videos, and blogs constantly, I found no shortage of material for my research. We were swimming in examples of real people doing #vanlife. The idea began to take concrete shape.

THE PLAN: Buy a small cargo van to be our daily driver, throw a mattress in the back along with our camping gear, and off we would go as soon as Jim started his summer break.

This plan could work because I could work from anywhere. Jim needed to be in Salt Lake City to grade AP essays mid-June, and so we would arrange our trip around that stay. We would head west from Atlanta, camping each night on the way to SLC, and head back across to the Great Lakes after the AP reading. We would turn south from there and return home through Ohio, Kentucky, and Tennessee.

That was the big idea anyway. Somehow, I convinced Jim we should sell our main car and buy a van. And then, the real planning started.

| 2 |

Lesson Two: Make a Map

Now we knew where we were.

We knew a little bit about where we wanted to go, and how we wanted to get there. But we needed a map.

If there are all kinds of ways to describe your location, there are just as many kinds of maps. We may map out a career path, a financial plan, or a route to do our weekly errands to save time and gas. As we got started mapping out exactly what our trips would look like, we quickly realized that there were a whole lot of ways to get from here to there. How could we possibly choose which way to go and which kinds of maps to use?

The distance between the point A of a big idea and the point B of actually hitting the road involved months of planning, some shopping, and more spreadsheets than you can imagine.

Our planning started with that germ of an idea mentioned in the previous chapter. Once a dream comes into view, the mind tends to focus on it, and ours were no different. Our conversations and imaginations became focused on three questions:

A - What roads should we take from Atlanta to SLC?
B - Where should we stop for the night along the way?
C - Where in the heck were we going to get a suitable van?

Of course, it was not so methodical as all that. All the choices and options in front of us overwhelmed our brains. How do you plan a trip somewhere you've never been in a van you don't yet own? Where to even start?

Google, of course.

The Van

Of all these, C seemed the most important (no van trip without a van), so we started with googling "camping in a small van," which led us to Facebook groups, blogs, and YouTube videos about camping in small vans. The vans we liked best were small cargo vans, and the options were Ford Transit Express, Nissan NV200, Chevy City Express (a rebrand of the Nissan, same exact vehicle underneath, though), and RAM ProMaster City.

The prevalence of Express and City in the names was apt, as these vans were easy to park and drive. This was key as our new van would become Jim's daily driver. I generally kept an old beater around for errands since I worked from home, but the new van would become our commute and travel vehicle for a few years, at least.

We kept an eye out for any vans like those for sale in our area. We were leaning toward the NV200 because of a Youtuber we followed who lived in one full time while traveling and hiking around the country. Another advantage to the NV200 was that a local company, Scampervan, had professionally converted some of these to campervans, allowing us to try one out for a night.

We rented a Scampervan for an overnight trip to a campground on the shores of Lake Lanier. Not too far from home, but far enough to get a feel for it on the road and in camp. The van was dropped off in our driveway by a helpful staff member who showed us all the bells and whistles. We learned how to raise the pop top, how to use the installed sink and cabinetry, and how to turn the back seat into a small double bed.

Soon enough, we were driving up I-85 in our home for the night. Arriving in late afternoon, it was still light outside, and we had no trouble setting up. A few unfamiliar things challenged us, like backing into the campsite at the correct angle, and figuring out the water hookup. Otherwise, it was a breeze. The bed was small and hard, but we slept fine. Our dog Poppy wasn't quite sure where to be but soon settled in the niche created under the front end of the bed. The cool night air encouraged us to snuggle, making the small bed just right.

Only one night of van camping and we were hooked.

Now set on the NV200, we had some ideas for a "no-build" setup that would solve some of the space and comfort challenges we experienced in the Scampervan. Avoiding installation of cabinetry would also allow us to have a queen size bed and full cargo capacity for hauling furniture and home and garden supplies. This approach to #vanlife would also lock in our van's utility as a work vehicle for resale. The hunt for our van began in earnest.

We found a listing for a 2017 Chevy City Express (remember, this was the NV200 rebranded). One model year old but brand new, it had failed to sell the year before. I detoured to see it on the way to a family visit. The salesman at the dealership may have thought me odd, the way I lay down in the back of the cargo van after the test drive. Once I saw the room it provided, including headroom that allowed me to stand most of the way upright, I was sold.

We went back to the car lot together to make our purchase. After the eternal process of dealership paperwork, we drove home in our first ever brand new vehicle. Our van. Our tiny home on wheels. No turning back now.

10 - ANNA AND JIM HALL

2017 Chevy City Express. Our little home on wheels.

A Place to Lay our Heads

We had a van and a general idea of how we wanted to go west from Atlanta. This felt like real progress. But an empty van isn't campground-ready, so we had to design the space we would live in while on the road and decide what items we couldn't live without on our journey.

What do you use on a normal day in your life?

For me, it's my toothbrush, toothpaste, soap, shampoo, towels, hairbrush, blow dryer, fresh clean clothes, shoes, food for breakfast, lunch, dinner, snacks, access to a computer, smartphone, books, TV, puzzles, musical instruments, containers of dog food, leashes, dog beds, our own bed, pillows, blankets, medicines, and white noise machine.

That about captures our normal daily needs. I like to think we are fairly minimalist people, but after making that list, I'm not so sure. How to fit all of that for two people and two dogs into a tiny van? That's where things get interesting.

Getting a van ready for camping can mean many things. Some people build beds and cabinetry into the van permanently to meet their needs. For us, we chose the "no-build" option which means everything would be removable. We chose lightweight items, easy to move in and out.

Measuring

The first step in preparing our van was getting an idea of just how much space we had to work with. Measuring every dimension and drawing out some sketches in an online room layout program helped us get a feel for how much room things would take up in the van.

Sleeping

Within those measurements, we first concentrated on sleeping. Wanting to avoid the hard and segmented bed experience of the

Scampervan, we decided that a plush foam mattress on the floor of the van would ensure our sleeping comfort. We bought a tri-fold foam mattress from Amazon, and it was the same width of the van. Laid completely out, it left only a little room at the back doors for anything else. But we figured out that we could fold one section in half to make a little pillow, creating a bed that was long enough for us to sleep comfortably while allowing more room at the end for all the stuff we might need at night.

All set up. You can just see the folded mattress and Poppy in her dog bed on top.

Storage

For storage, we added two plastic dressers. One smaller one would be for camping and kitchen stuff, and the larger one held our clothes. These fit in the back of the van facing each other, so we could access them from inside or out. We often moved these out of the van and under our awning, tarp or small tent at night to give us more room in the van, so the plastic kept things light and easy to rearrange. We secured them with straps while traveling. A quick release, and they were ready to be moved out when we needed to reclaim the space in the van.

Cooking

For cooking, we had done some camping before and had butane burners. In the past, car camping in a tent, we used full sized skillets from home, but our tiny storage drawers meant any new supplies were the smallest and lightest ones, often designed for backpacking. We bought a tiny nested set of pots and pans with handles that folded in for them most compact storage. We brought our rice cooker from home, which just fit in our bottom kitchen drawer, and which we used more than anything else on our trip. We packed a few additional utensils and cooking accessories from home, and that was about it. We did not have a fridge in the van, and so primarily depended on shelf-stable ingredients for meals, such as rice, beans, canned chicken, salmon pouches, and canned vegetables. Snacks included fruit, chips, cereal, and protein bars. We also brought a cooler for cold drinks and occasional cold groceries.

Interior of van. Drawers are still inside the house for packing.

Layout

While driving, we folded up the mattress into couch form which allowed room to lounge during daytime rest stops. The crate could sit along one side and doubled as a table as needed for rainy day meals. The back section stayed set up with dressers, the cooler, and our camping potty in case of emergency pit stops.

At night, we planned to take out the crate and at least one of the dressers, fold out the mattress, and move the cooler to the front seat. That would give us room to move around while getting ready for bed and settling down for the night.

Décor

Once all that was settled, I couldn't resist blinging things up. I sewed a navy and white printed fabric into black out curtains that would attach to the ceiling and walls with magnetized hooks. I also fashioned a custom header out of foam insulation and decorative vinyl, but that ended up going by the wayside in favor of the extra two inches of headroom. I bought bedding in coordinating blue fabrics and set everything up for an Insta-ready photo op. It never looked that good again.

Personal Care

In the top smallest drawer of our clothes dresser, we packed a minimal set of toiletries to get us through the trip. Sample sizes took up less room, and we knew we could replace them as needed if we ran out. We are pretty low-maintenance, so this worked for us.

Dog supplies

The dogs were one of the hardest things to plan around. They could sleep with us at night, but need to be in the crate for riding. They needed bowls, food, treats, leashes and harnesses, and that took up more room than we expected. We ended up sticking with small bags of food and just resupplying as needed, and dedicating one drawer to their needs in our kitchen/camping dresser. The crate rode in the van during travel, but we put it out at night to have room for sleeping.

Testing it out

We still needed to test it out in a real camping situation. We took the newly outfitted van to Black Rock Mountain State Park in north Georgia. Set up was easy, but we soon realized that leaving doors open while getting situated after dark could let in a few bugs. A gigantic and scary one joined us in the van right at bedtime, which made for some interesting gymnastics and aerobics until the situation was resolved. That lesson behind us, we had a great rest of the night. Our love for #vanlife only grew. The sheer pleasure of camping in a beautiful place was amplified by our pride in creating our little van habitat.

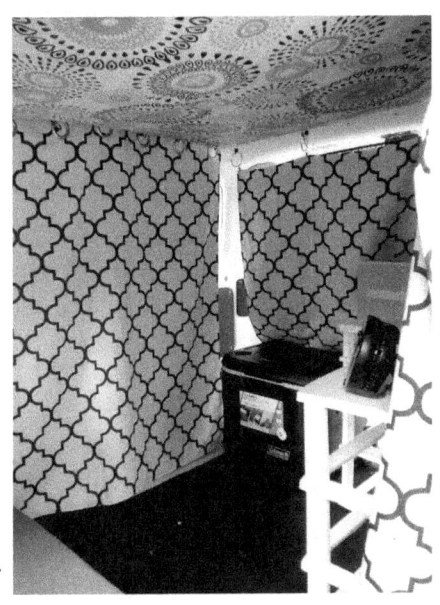
Interior of van.

We were ready to hit the road. Or so we thought.

Best Laid Plans

An old saying asserts that anything which can go wrong, will go wrong. It's not been my experience in life in general. But there were times that metaphorical speed bumps or sinkholes threatened to run us right off the road as we approached our van trips.

Somehow, our new puppy managed to break her leg at doggy daycare. That got expensive. The trip fund shrank. But we rebuilt it.

Work and church situations consumed us with phone calls and emails as we tried to get the van and ourselves packed for that first long day of driving. We took turns working and packing until all of both were done.

The very morning we left the second year, our dogs scrapped over some food as Jim was packing their gear for the trip. Jim's leg got a minor injury in the fray. Some first aid and packing some extra antibiotic ointment helped us stay on track.

No matter what, we persisted. And I think that's the key factor in all of this. Don't let the things that might run someone else off the road get you sidetracked. Just keep moving forward.

Where to?

As we persisted through these minor detours, we tackled the final tasks: laying out the precise routes of our travels and figuring out where we would camp each night. We worked on the route first. Knowing how many nights we'd be camping in a row, and how many breaks we would take in other accommodations, would help us decide the best spots to sleep.

If you are planning a cross-country road trip, you may want to do what we did, or not. Sometimes having everything planned out ahead of time was a relief. Other times, we canceled planned reservations to take off after a new possibility. All in all, I'll say that having a plan meant we could always change it, but on the rare occasions we struck forward without any plan, the stress of where we would stay that night often overshadowed our enjoyment of that day's adventures.

So here are two methods we used to plan:

Over-planning Method

1. Plug a starting point and ending point into Google Maps
2. Figure out how long to drive each day. For us the sweet spot is 4 hours or less, although we've certainly pushed it further when we needed to cover a lot of distance quickly.
3. Look at the detailed steps in the maps program or website to break it into appropriately timed segments.

4. Take a look at what towns or cities are near the ends of each segment. One year, with the longer legs of travel, it went something like this: Atlanta-Kentucky-Missouri-Eastern Nebraska-Western Nebraska-Middle Wyoming-Western Wyoming-Salt Lake City-Western Wyoming-Northeastern Wyoming-Southwestern Minnesota-Northeastern Minnesota-Wisconsin-UP Michigan-Eastern Michigan-Southern Michigan-Ohio-Kentucky-Tennessee-Atlanta. The next year we took our time, so it was Atlanta-Mississippi-Arkansas-Kansas City-Iowa-Sioux Falls-Middle South Dakota-Bismarck-Western North Dakota-Montana-Manitoba-Northeastern Minnesota-UP Michigan-Green Bay-Springfield-Paducah-Nashville-Atlanta.
5. Get out travel guides, detailed maps and websites, and make a list of sights and attractions near those stopping points. We focused on dog-friendly places, so mostly state and national parks and historic sites, with the occasional museum thrown in if we had time to take turns watching the dogs in the parking lot.
6. Book campsites at those stopping points, or lodging if a better option and in the budget.
7. Be prepared for those plans to change. One year a heat wave and a minor injury meant choosing cool clean hotels for a few days. Another year a little sign about the Laura Ingalls Wilder Homeplace shifted our route completely. Tornado watches sometimes meant choosing a camping cabin rather than a campsite for safety reasons. The need for Wi-Fi and a place to do focused work changed our plans one night from a minimalist campground to a RV park with a rec room. Hold all plans loosely and you can roll with the waves.
8. Keep an eye on cancellation requirements. We only lost one night's fees to a cancellation, but have learned only to pre-book those that are cancellable up until arrival. You never know when you may see a once-in-a-lifetime opportunity on a little sign by the side of the road and have to detour from your original plans.

Under-planning Method

1. Figure out where you want to end up.
2. Start driving in that direction.
3. Stop at any attractions that look interesting.
4. When you get tired, look for a campground or book some lodging.

As you can see, the second method is much less work. It also takes the fun out of research and planning. The worst part is how it makes us hyper-focused toward the end of the day on booking something, or coping with the constant nagging concern we might not find a suitable place for the night. It's hard to enjoy anything else with that on our minds. The more experience we get, though, the more we are able to spot where a place may have ample availability, so we can just show up, and the more we make sure all reservations are cancellable in case of those unexpected changes in plans.

We have some preferences when it comes to where we sleep. While many vanlifers prefer free off-the-beaten-path campsites, either stealth or on dispersed camping areas or publicly accessible lands, we like a few more amenities.

This means choosing state or national parks, private campgrounds, or other serviced campsites where possible. We like clean bathrooms with showers, electricity to charge everything, and running water at least somewhere nearby for cooking and cleaning.

Our favorite campsites have been small independent private campgrounds. They often have facilities up to par with a KOA or other chain, but are less crowded and noisy. The uniqueness is also a plus, because a campsite may be next to a farm with animals or on the edge of beautiful trails for hiking.

Campsite, Phillips RV Park, Evanston, WY

Other favorite campsites have been in parks, whether state, national, or city/county-owned. They tend to be more basic in restroom facilities and amenities, but the connection to trails, historic sites, and ranger programs can offer lots of exploring without ever having to move the van.

Campsite, City Park, Adrian, Minnesota

Finally, our tried and true option is KOA. We are members of their discount club, and while the uniformity might not be for everyone, during a stressful leg of the trip, knowing exactly what to expect in terms of service and amenities can be a relief. And being a chain doesn't prevent unexpected delights like the seemingly infinite bunnies in Douglas, WY, or the fun of seeing our dogs frolic with friends in their K9 dog parks.

Campsite, KOA, Eureka Springs, Arkansas

If you are planning your first cross-country camping trip and have the resources to afford it, we would suggest starting out at a KOA for a more "glamping" experience, then booking a few nights at a state or national park, then trying out some less serviced city/county or Good Sam independent campgrounds. Maybe at that point you'll be ready for some dispersed options and even stealth camping. I'm not sure if we will ever do the stealth thing, but we do have our eye on some public dispersed camping for future adventures.

Into the Unknown

The most challenging thing about planning and preparing for #vanlife was grappling with how much we couldn't know. We didn't know how expensive things would really be on the road. We didn't know how the weather would affect our driving or sleeping along the way. We didn't know how we would get along in such a small space with so few creature comforts over so long a journey. We really didn't know if we would even complete the journey as planned. One or both of us could get sick. Or one or both of the dogs. The van could break down. Work could get in the way. It was all so... unpredictable.

The biggest challenge of preparing for #vanlife was learning to live in that unpredictable territory. It was also the biggest gift.

At the end of all this planning, we pointed the van north one hot morning in late May. Driving through the Atlanta suburbs into the exurbs and soon enough into the foothills of Appalachia, we looked at each other with bleary eyes, astounded that we were really doing this. Finally emerging from the suburbs into the country, the road stretched ahead of us dotted only with a few other cars. We had come too far to turn back now.

We didn't stop until a little past Chattanooga, TN, where we found a gas station on our side of the road that seemed easy to pull in and out. It wasn't much of a gas station, honestly. Not one of the fancy plazas with big clean restrooms and lots of food choices like we typically preferred, but the older kind, with basic snacks, gas, and a simple bathroom. What set it apart, though, was a giant rock face abutting the parking lot. The way the road had been carved out of the mountain was evident in this steep dark wall of jagged rocks.

The gas station had made the most of its natural setting. Each ridge that stuck out far enough held a painted rock. The painted rocks featured art, messages, slogans, initials, anything you might imagine. Signs cautioned to not get too close, so it seemed as though placing new rocks might be discouraged. I didn't have a rock or paint, so I simply stood and took them all in.

Looking up and down the wall, I noticed, right in the middle about halfway up, a rock painted with the Mystery Machine van from Scooby Doo. Perfect. We peeled out, hoping to make Kentucky by suppertime, so we wouldn't have to set up our first campsite in the dark. The Mystery Machine felt like a good sign for this first day of #vanlife.

A sign that in this van, on this road, was exactly where we belonged.

Rock Wall, Twice Daily Gas Station, Kimball, Tennessee

| 3 |

Lesson Three: Cross Your Rubicon

We got to our first campsite in Land of Lakes, Kentucky, just before dark. The location was as scenic as the name implies. Our campsite sat on the edge of sapphire blue waters, tall pines separating it from the campsites on either side. I was thankful for a little privacy from other campers for this, our first setup of the trip. Just in case it devolved into chaos.

Happy with this prime campsite for our first night on the road, we tumbled out of the van. Jim took our dog, Poppy, for a quick walk and then stood by the van, unsure of what to do first. I appraised our situation in light of my practice sessions setting up the van in the driveway.

OK, I thought. Here we go.

We took turns hauling things out of the van, with the one not on duty holding Poppy. We discovered that lakeside camping involves many mosquitos. Many, many, mosquitos.

We took turns hiking to the bathhouse a football field away, sorely needed by that point. The humid air pressed in on us even as the sky edged toward twilight. Kentucky is still in the south, though a day's drive north of our own muggy Georgia.

Sweat poured into our eyes as we continued the Tetris game of moving things in and out. Finally, inside the van, we had an unfolded and made bed, our clothes container and the camping potty at the foot of the bed, and our backpack of devices and the cooler in the two front seats. Outside, we had a tarp awning going off the side of the van with our kitchen dresser and bins underneath. That first night's awning set up was the best of our trip. By the next year, we had attached a manufactured awning. But that night, I got it just as I had practiced, tight between the van and the poles, precisely enough slope to avoid any puddling of dew or water, and it looked sharp, if I may say so myself.

I attached the window screens I had designed with magnets to keep bugs out and allow air in, as well as a set of magnetic hooks and curtain to block off the potty area at the foot of the bed. I placed the Reflectix window coverings I had customized on the windows to allow us sun protection in the morning and privacy from other campers at night. Almost done. Sweaty, miserable, getting very hungry, but almost done.

The final step was setting a window air conditioner on top of the kitchen dresser under the awning, rigged up so the frigid air blew through a crack in one of the front windows. An all weather extension cord ran from the campsite electric to the van with the power strip hung inside that cracked window, for powering the AC and charging our many other devices. We might have been camping, but we definitely weren't off the grid.

Once we piled back in to sit on our bed and eat some sandwiches in the blissful cool of the air conditioning, we realized — we could have had the van running the whole time and set everything up with cool air blowing from the vehicle air conditioning. Oops. Lesson learned.

But we didn't kill each other, we made it work, and had a great first night's sleep in our cool and cozy van. I'd call that a successful first night on the road.

The next morning, we stumbled out of our very cold van into the day. The windows were opaque with thick condensation. After taking turns at the bathhouse and walking Poppy, we opened the back doors of the van and gazed at the foggy lake while our breakfast bars and diet soda brought us back to life.

Many Rivers to Cross

The two rivers surrounding us on our first night out on the road were just the beginning of the relationship we would develop with rivers along our journey. Land of Lakes is a series of hydroelectric dammed lakes on the Tennessee and Cumberland rivers. The intersection between the two rivers is a peninsula larger than any other in the inland United States. A fact which we only discovered on a marker as we headed out of the area.

Honestly, we didn't even consider when planning our trip how many rivers we would cross. We knew we were voyaging across the country, across many states, traveling from our eastern city to beyond the Rockies, and basically from south to north to south across the entire continent. But rivers were not on our mind.

During the first few hundred miles, rivers were barely visible to us. Of course, they were everywhere, if we had known where to look. The first river we crossed was the Chattahoochee just north of Atlanta, followed quickly by the Etowah up near Cartersville, the waters of both a blur off the side of the road as we navigated the fast traffic of multiple-lane interstates. We also crossed the Oostanaula as we passed through Resaca, but didn't notice that one and had honestly never heard of it. We only realized it existed when we saw it later in our Georgia Gazetteer.

But the first river that made an impression on us was the Tennessee. Driving along its broad waters near Chattanooga, it felt like a starting ribbon, like we were really on our way up and out of the south.

Now, rolling onto the arched I-24 bridge across the broad brown Ohio River after our night at Land of Lakes, sausage biscuits in hand, we began to sense that rivers were going to be our constant companion.

Why didn't we realize this before? Good question. I think that when we don't see it on a daily basis, we forget how connected we are and have necessarily been to the natural world. Industry and travel today take place by air, road, and rail. We have no need to depend on the waterways to get what we want, to go where we want, so we have developed an amnesia around their very existence.

Rivers, though, are like the arterial systems that enliven our bodies and connect everything that gives us life. Rivers form a map of how people lived in and on our continent for thousands of years. All people, all cultures, all industries this land has held over the last hundred and fifty years have been intertwined with our river system. And now our journey was woven into that tapestry as well.

Mississippi Crossings

Take the Mississippi, for example. The O.G. Big River. Legendary in song and story throughout the history of our continent. That first year, we crossed the big river in St. Louis. After the interstate highway rises through countless railroad tracks intermingled with brushy landscape to cross the river, the narrow two lanes of westward traffic move fast and prevent any good look at the wide muddy waters. You can take a quick look at the Gateway Arch, that giant metal monument built in honor of Westward Expansion, if a semi-truck doesn't get in the way. Industry fills both sides as the road hits solid ground again. A frantic search for signs indicating the correct lane through St. Louis means looking backward toward the river feels as dangerous as being Lot's wife. An underwhelming experience, to say the least.

Gateway Arch, from Merchants Bridge across the Mississippi River, St. Louis, Missouri

Crossing the Mississippi in Memphis, as we did the following year, made us very happy, but that was mostly due to the bellies full of BBQ we carried over into Arkansas. A pedestrian bridge, a welcome addition for walkers, blocks any good views of the river to the north. But looking south, if you are fortunate enough to find a long enough gap between the oncoming traffic, you might see a river that stretches out languidly and rounds into a wider curve beyond.

Even when we don't see it very well, crossing the Mississippi feels like we are officially "out west." While Missouri and Arkansas are still hot, humid, and buggy, they beckon us forward toward cooler, drier, wide open spaces beyond.

Experiencing the Mississippi as a border between our homeland and the lands beyond suits its history. The river changed hands often between indigenous and European nations and served as a border between them until the Louisiana Purchase just over 200 years ago. The name, Misi-ziibi, means Great River in Ojibwe, and Native Americans lived along it for thousands of years before Europeans knew it existed. By the 1600s C.E., European fur traders, priests, and explorers traveled and traded along the river. From the Mississippian tribes at Cahokia, to the French, Spanish, British, and eventually, the United States, the shifting possession and exploration of the river created a beautiful tapestry of diversity. The river's gifts of agriculture, trade, and transit continue to sustain those that live along it and the rest of the country.

As much as the Mississippi symbolizes our going beyond our normal southern confines, we never see the crossing heading back east. Lovers of the Great Lakes, we always head home through Minnesota and Wisconsin and Michigan. Up that far, the great river is just another little waterway, with headwaters only a few feet across. You can stop in Lake Itasca, MN to visit these headwaters, but we never have. Maybe next time.

Bluffs and Blunders

On our second night of #vanlife, now well west of the Mississippi and weary from over 6 hours of hard driving, we arrived at our next campsite. Arrow Rock, Missouri, is a state historic site that preserves a historic town along the Missouri River. The high bluff holding the town was a stopping point for people along the river throughout history, from indigenous Americans to explorers to early settlers. However, the population peaked in Arrow Rock around the time of the Civil War and by the 20th century held only a few hundred people. By the time we visited, less than 100 people called Arrow Rock home. In addition to some historical markers, the village contains a historic tavern, two or three gift shops, and a few bed and breakfast lodgings. We only drove through the town outside of business hours so can't testify to their interest or quality, but it was a cute little place.

Our campsite in a park next to the village was off the beaten path, historic, and picturesque -- everything we look for in our travels. After checking in with the campground host, we parked the van in our home for the night. Oak giants met each other far overhead and sheltered ours and every other site in deep shade. Bird songs filled the air. We congratulated each other on another perfect sleep spot.

The air was muggy and buggy, just like at Land of Lakes, but I had learned my lesson and left the van running as I unpacked. The cool AC made everything easier. Jim walked Poppy while I began setting up our campsite.

I unloaded the outdoor gear, and began trying to rig up the tarp awning. It sagged no matter what I tried, but since it wasn't raining, I let it go. We would need the window air again that night as things didn't get one degree cooler as night approached. However, if we wanted to park as we had initially, with our back doors open to the scenic woods for that perfect #vanlife picture, the campsite electricity was on the wrong side of the van for our cord to reach the AC unit. Oops.

Ok, I'd improvise — I rigged up a second tarp on the other side of the van to shelter our clothes dresser with AC unit on top, blowing deliciously cold and dehumidified air through the screened window into our sleeping space. I was slapping mosquitos off my body constantly, so we enjoyed dinner at our campsite picnic table in a fragrant cloud of bug spray.

The deep shade of the tree canopy brought twilight to us well before the sun had truly set, which was fine with our tired bodies. We piled back into the van to sleep.

Unfortunately, I had decided to use our clothes dresser to support the window AC, since the kitchen dresser was on the side of the van nearer the picnic table. I didn't think anything of it because I was planning to sleep in the t-shirt and leggings I had worn all day. Jim began grabbing a few toiletries to visit the bathhouse, where he also planned to change into his softer clothes for sleeping. He asked where those clothes had ended up. They were in the dresser. Oops again.

I instructed him to open the drawers very carefully to get them out, as the AC was sitting precariously on top. In hindsight, I should have gotten out of the van and held the AC in place while he opened the drawers. But I was tired and all comfy in bed. My comfiness ended with a loud crash as the AC unit plummeted to the ground.

I leapt out of the van to see what was going on. The AC lay on the ground upside down, still blowing its cold air but now aimed under the van. I hadn't realized how tired I was until I began sobbing at the sight of it. Many accusations and recriminations followed between us as we worked to get everything set back up and prayed that the AC unit had not been damaged beyond use. The cold air blew into the van again, and we gave thanks for small miracles.

Once all that was done, I was so mad and keyed up I didn't even want to get back in the van. But you can't go for a drive to mentally cool off when your vehicle is your house and all set up for sleeping. Walking in air thick with bugs and humidity was not going to cool me off physically or mentally. I felt trapped.

I resigned myself to my lot and got back in the van. I couldn't even get in the front seats with the van set up for sleeping, so I sat on the center console, as far away from Jim and the dogs as I could manage, with my body contorted between the front seats. If I could, I would have folded myself up and gotten in the floorboards just to be alone for a while. Bent toward it like a pretzel, I let the cool air from the AC unit blow directly on the back of my neck. Jim was kind enough to leave me alone while I cooled down and processed. After an hour or so, the quiet and cool brought me back down to earth, and I was ready to rejoin society. Society had fallen asleep by that point, so I pulled out my Kindle and lay down alongside to hopefully join him in slumber before too long.

The next morning the campground had filled with a thick fog. We awoke snuggly, calmer, and content. The birds serenaded us, a beautiful alarm clock to get us going for the day. The cool foggy air in the dawn light wrapped us in blissful softness. We had slain the dragon of camping stress and made it through the night. The pictures we took that morning of the fog-soft woods framed by our van's back doors were the epitome of Insta-perfect #vanlife. Appearances (especially online) can be quite deceiving.

Van life isn't always fun and instagrammable. Two nights in, and we had already experienced and survived our first camping "disaster."

The truth is somewhere between the stress of the night before and the peaceful beauty of the morning after. Driving through the streets of Arrow Rock for a final look, the fog made an impressionist painting of the buildings and I wished we could stay longer to explore. But we had to keep moving to make it to Salt Lake City in good time. Thankful for short memories of stress and long memories of scenery, we moved on down the road.

Fellow Travelers

After Arrow Rock, the Missouri River and the Lewis and Clark National Historic Trail were our constant companions. While the Mississippi may be the most famous of the rivers we crossed, the Missouri was the most present on our journeys. The Missouri River begins in snow melt streams pouring off the Rocky Mountains that join in Three Forks, Montana and ends in its juncture with the Mississippi in St. Louis, Missouri. Heading upstream, as we did, the Missouri River traverses Missouri, Kansas, Iowa, Nebraska, South Dakota, North Dakota, and then Montana.

Missouri River, Fort Mandan, North Dakota

It is, in fact, the longest river in North America, and we would eventually wonder how it was possible to cross one river so many times. We crossed it in numerous states, in small river towns, larger river cities, and empty countryside. The ever-present Missouri, somehow taking the same route west as our little van.

That's not a coincidence. The major travel routes from east to west across our continent were shaped by the trails of indigenous peoples, their explorations such as that of the Yazoo explorer Monchacht-Ape, and the later expedition of Lewis and Clark to the Pacific along the Missouri. The Lewis and Clark expedition hoped that the Missouri river would provide a northwest passage to the Pacific Ocean. While we weren't trying to find a river passage to the Pacific ourselves, we crossed paths with the route of Lewis and Clark almost as many times as we crossed the Missouri.

Lewis and Clark Animatronics, Lewis and Clark Interpretive Center, Sioux City, Iowa

We first found ourselves on the Lewis and Clark Route in St. Louis, although we passed through so fast we didn't notice. The bluffs at Arrow Rock were an early stop on their expedition, and held a historical marker that launched a casual quest to visit all the Lewis and Clark sites we could along our travels.

In Sioux City, Iowa, we visited the Lewis and Clark Interpretive Center to learn more about their voyage. Animatronics brought the main characters of the journey to life, including Thomas Jefferson, who gave them their marching orders, Meriwether Lewis, William Clark, the African-American named York who was a slave of William Clark, and essential translator Sacagawea and less helpful husband/enslaver Toussaint Charbonneau. Our favorite animatronic, though, was that of

Meriwether Lewis' dog, Seaman, who would be with them all the way to the Pacific Coast and back. Seaman was such a loyal companion that he is said to have stopped eating after Lewis died and died of grief at his grave.

Further north, in Fort Mandan, North Dakota, we learned more about how Sacagawea and Charbonneau joined the expedition and saw the bleak winter encampment fort where the party survived against all odds.

Fort Mandan State Historic Site, Washburn, North Dakota

And in Chamberlain, South Dakota, the Dignity sculpture overlooking the Missouri River took our breath away. Standing tall over the flat land and river bluffs, her metal cloak appears as stained-glass, catching the sun and lighting up in blue and white and silver. Designed by Dale Claude Lamphere and David Claymore, she is only 6 years old but feels ancient. We first thought it was a representation of Sacagawea herself, fitting for our Lewis and Clark explorations, but soon discovered that she was her own woman, intended to honor the Lakota and Dakota cultures indigenous to the lands on which she stands. This giantess was our watcher and protector as we walked the grounds beneath her gaze, her cloak soaring over us like a shield.

Under Dignity's watchful eye, the Lewis and Clark Interpretive and Keelboat Center taught us about the ship that got the explorers as far as North Dakota. However, sitting where it did under Dignity brought to life how, without Sacagawea's assistance and translation, their journey would have been impossible.

Between and along the Mississippi, the Missouri, and countless other rivers like the Platte, the Yellowstone, the Minnesota, we drove across the native lands of more tribes than I could have imagined. Starting with our time gazing up at Dignity, we worked to learn about these people, many wiped out by the need for land at the center of American expansion. An expansion made possible, in many cases, by those tribes and the rivers that were sacred waters to these tribes. An expansion that cost many American Indians their lives, livelihoods and lands. Yet they have worked to keep their river stories alive.

Dignity of Earth and Sky, Chamberlain, South Dakota

River Stories

The river stories of Native Americans and notable explorers like Lewis and Clark are depicted in seemingly infinite exhibits and historical markers. But we all have river stories, even if they are not depicted in a museum.

As we crossed waterway after waterway, I kept thinking of a favorite album called *American River*. This sound and word poem celebrates rivers in an almost sacred way. On the song, "The Continuance" Johnny and Roseanne Cash tell their river story, which is deeply linked to the Mississippi Delta that nourished the farmland of Johnny's early life. All of us, just by the very land we inhabit, we each have at least one river story.

Sioux Falls, Big Sioux River, South Dakota

At a conference on ecology and faith last year, a speaker asked us to introduce ourselves by saying which watershed we hail from. The waters we drink, that water our plants, that wash down our streets all flow toward some larger body of water. For me and my house, that is the South Fork Peachtree Creek that flows into the Chattahoochee. The Chattahoochee then flows all the way down to the Gulf of Mexico at Apalachicola Bay. This watershed is mine. I grew up only a couple of hours north of Apalachicola. As a kid, nothing compared to a drive down to see the ocean and enjoy some oysters made delicious by the meeting of fresh and salt waters in the bay. Those oysters are endangered now from storm damage, pollution and over-harvesting. A restoration plan is in place, but it remains to be seen how effective it will be. That is one of my river stories.

Former U.S. President Jimmy Carter said of the rivers in the southwest Georgia homeland that we share,

> "My journey as an environmentalist began in the rivers and creeks around my home. Since our ancestors moved into southwest Georgia, our family farm has been nourished by Choctahatchee and Kinchafoonee creeks, and for more than 80 years I have relished and enjoyed these watersheds. A lifetime of fishing, swimming and birding has helped me learn firsthand that all aspects of our lives are tied to the health of our free-flowing streams."

Those watersheds are part of his river story, and a part of mine.

Those who live on the other side of the railroad tracks near my house splash in puddles that flow into the South River, which flows into the Ocmulgee, which bends and turns until it joins the Altamaha and flows into the Atlantic Ocean north of St. Simons Island. As a kid, one of my sacred spaces was a forked tree alongside the marsh on the Georgia coast where I would sit and read and observe birds. The salt marsh aquatic ecosystem remains a source of sustenance and shelter for many plants and animals. Salt marshes are lost daily to development and rising sea levels, so constant vigilance is required by preservation groups to keep these ecosystems safe. This is also part of my river story.

We all have river stories. What is yours? What lessons does it have for you?

Perhaps the best lesson we learned from the rivers along our trip was this: There was no place we stood or drove that was not first useful and sacred to the generations before us. When we ignore the voices of those earlier generations and current river peoples, we dishonor the gifts of the rivers.

When we broaden our view, we remember who was first in this land. We remember that we can't own creation, and that we exploit it at our peril. We remember those parts of our spirit that come alive when connected to our natural world.

We were created as part of these natural systems which we forget so easily.

When we forget all this, we are less than whole people. We are less than we can be. We are less than we were created to be.

The gift of travel, especially travel that brings us close to people, close to the water, close to the land, close to the sky, is how it helps us remember.

A Reminder to Remember

Out in middle America on a two-lane blacktop, it was hard to tell what we were seeing as traffic slowed to a crawl. From a distance, we could see a few cars backed up out in the middle of nowhere on a country road. Some police lights flickered blue and white beyond them. Had there been a wreck? Was a car stalled out and blocking traffic? As we drew closer, the scene came into focus.

Lake waters lapped up onto the roadway. From our perspective, the yellow lines of the lanes disappeared into gray for about a football field's distance before rising on the other side. The sun glittered off the wind-raised mini-waves undulating up the pavement. The pleasant sunny weather held no hint of the heavy rains the week before.

We stared at each other in disbelief. We were not going to make it down this back road as planned.

Oh, we had heard about flooding in some of the Midwestern states, but that didn't stop us from our usual backroads explorations. As we hadn't encountered any flood damage or detours, it was easy to imagine it was all over by the time we got west of the Mississippi. The error of that thinking was now covering the road ahead of us.

We sat in the line of cars for some time once we realized the situation. Should we turn around? Should we wait? One by one, cars turned around out of line to drive past us in the other direction. Each defector from the queue helped us make our decision. We joined them, making our five-point turn and retreating back the way we had come.

As we used our phone GPS despite spotty service to figure out an alternate route, we talked about what we had seen. Threats like flooding are increasing in the Midwest, and around the world. At the Dinosaur Museum in Dickinson, North Dakota, they had a little interactive sandbox, where you could move the sand to model different topographies. A projection displayed what areas would be underwater in various scenarios of sea level rise. Almost all projections were pretty bad news for most of the coasts, and lots of river valleys as well. We had seen the future on that back road.

The river beauty along our trip was ever-present. The threat was there too, but easy to forget. Once the flood detour lay behind us, our minds and conversations quickly turned to new adventures ahead.

| 4 |

Lesson Four: Be a Stranger in a Strange Land

Driving down a narrow two-lane road in Nebraska that bisected prairie as far as the eye could see, it was easy to understand how some would call this part of the country boring. For me, though, the long views across fields toward far-off scrubby tree lines, dotted only by the occasional farmhouse or tractor, made room for my imagination. My mind conjured up images of us as pioneers as we pressed "Westward Ho!" Those pioneers who traveled westward in covered wagons to settle the parts of our country beyond the original colonies were brave and resourceful like us, in our American mythology at least. The iconic images learned in grade school stay with you. My brain has an entire section filled with episodes of *Little House on the Prairie* and old westerns seen on the Superstation every day during those latchkey kid hours until my mom got home. Maybe some memories of dying of dysentery in the *Oregon Trail* video game rattled around in there as well. The Cole Porter song, "Don't Fence Me In," popped into my head, with its glorious images of starry skies and murmuring cottonwood trees mirroring what we saw in real time.

Of course, I turned out to be allergic to cottonwood trees, but it does make for a romantic image.

Living Like Laura Ingalls

After a sign inspired us to take off across the prairie on a whim, we found, on another little country road in the middle of nowhere, the Ingalls Homestead in de Smet, South Dakota. This historical and cultural recreation of a pioneer homestead brought to life my childhood obsession with the *Little House on the Prairie* books and TV shows. (If you don't believe it rose to the level of obsession, just ask my parents about the time I lost Carrie from my *Little House on the Prairie* Colorforms toy set after she fell into the seat belt opening in my dad's old truck. I was inconsolable.)

At the homestead, I stepped wide-eyed into a world that I had only read, imagined, and seen on the small screen.

Ingalls Homestead, De Smet, South Dakota

Among the exhibits, the costumed reenactors, the barnyard animals, riding in the horse drawn wagon, and sitting for a lesson in the one room schoolhouse, I lived out my dreams of being Laura growing up on the prairie. We lucked out due to a cancellation and got a campsite on the farm. Around the campfire after supper, we sang happy birthday to a young girl whose family had taken her to see all the Laura Ingalls Wilder historic sites across the Midwest. We slept in our own modern-day covered wagon out under the stars. It was magical.

Ingalls Homestead, De Smet, South Dakota

We decided after our visit to watch a few episodes of the TV show, for old times' sake. We didn't get far into the pilot when the screen depicted two Native American men barging into the Ingalls house uninvited when Caroline was alone with the children. They tear apart some of her belongings, but due to the language barrier, it is not clear what they want. Only when she gives them Charles' tobacco do they go on their way. We have no way of knowing why they came to the house or what they wanted. All we learn is that our protagonists fear them. The framing and scoring of the scene makes it clear we are supposed to be scared for Caroline. The men are implied to be dangerous. They are framed as threats, as enemies. This scene brings to life the painful history of American Indians being seen as intruders on land where the Ingalls and other settlers were the true intruders.

Sod Dugout House, Ingalls Homestead, South Dakota

A display in the museum on the Ingalls homestead tells the real story. At first, the Ingalls attempted to settle in one area they thought had land for settlers. It later turned out that the US had no treaty for that land and the Ingalls necessarily moved on. Charles was angry and felt betrayed. But the Native Americans who had lived on that land experienced the first and ultimate betrayal, for despite treaties settled or unsettled, the white people came, forcing indigenous people off their homelands and even off areas where they had initially been relocated.

Beloved childhood literature, TV, and movies lose some of their shine when viewed with modern eyes. I still love the way The Little House on the Prairie made me feel as a child, and the renewal of that childlike wonder on our visit. But with adult eyes, I can now see the complexity in the pioneer narratives and am thankful for that more nuanced view.

Cottonwoods and Culture

In Chamberlain, South Dakota, during one of our many picnic lunches along the banks of the Missouri River, we found ourselves under attack from cottonwood trees seeking to spread their seeds. The fluffy seeds blew in our hair, our food, our drinks. A beautiful view was made unenjoyable by these tiny paratroopers. We decided to choose an indoor pastime instead.

The Akta Lakota Museum and Cultural Center sits not far from the river on the grounds of a school. Not knowing what to expect, we looked forward to learning more about the local tribes and maybe seeing some artifacts or folk arts of the native peoples. We got way more than we bargained for.

The Center is in a building on the campus of a school which began its life as a traditional Indian School. Such schools sought to remove the native cultures from their students and assimilate them into Eurocentric society. This approach produced tragic results, including abuse and death of students.

Akta Lakota Museum and Cultural Center, Chamberlain, South Dakota

Nowadays, the school serves American Indian students in need of support and services. The museum highlights the often tragic history of both the school and the local tribes in the area, while also emphasizing the persistent strength and beauty of the native peoples and their culture. A chapel on the grounds, rich with Native art and motifs, felt especially sacred, yet reminded me of all the ways Christianity was used to harm in the work of forced relocation and assimilation.

We left enlightened, disheartened, but also hopeful.

Finding the beauty that remains in the shadows of profound racism and injustice helped us remember not to characterize American Indians as singularly tragic figures or stereotypical spiritual guides only here to teach the rest of us. Their culture and experience is dynamic and nuanced, if we have eyes to see and ears to hear.

We Know We Belong to the Land

In the Rodgers and Hammerstein musical, *Oklahoma*, the cast sings, "We know we belong to the land." These fictional settlers, only on the land a generation or two at most, were part of displacing indigenous tribes who could claim many generations on it. Yet they felt a sense of belonging to the land already. I can confess a similar sense of deep belonging when I am on the land of my ancestors and family in southwest Georgia, although my family's history only reaches back as far as Creek Indian displacement in the early 1800s. While my feeling of belonging is real, it is complicated by the fact that, like the all-white cast of the movie version of *Oklahoma*, none of my ancestors had their possession of American lands disputed based on race or religion. It has been easy for me to believe in the romance of the frontier.

The stories of the Akta Lakota and other episodes from American history trouble simplistic notions of settling land and claiming wide open spaces. There were no empty frontiers. The romantic ideal of pioneers and cowboys ignores entire cultures that predated the "settlement" of these lands.

From the earliest European encounters on our soil, Native Americans were under threat. Diseases like smallpox brought by these newcomers decimated tribes. Only one in ten on average survived this onslaught of biological exposure. Settlers enslaved tribal peoples to build their early settlements. Tribes were recruited to join various military sides among the European powers battling over borders and died in these wars. By the 1830s, numerous broken treaties and the Indian Removal Act displaced tens of thousands, including the Creeks, forced off the land where my family settled in southwest Georgia a few years later.

On another frontier, in the early days of Texas, the Mexican government issued an invitation to Americans to move in and settle if they would agree to a few rules; become Mexican citizens and follow Mexican law (including no slavery), learn to speak Spanish, and convert to Catholicism. Americans poured into Texas by the thousands to take advantage of the opportunity. Yet they didn't want to follow the laws of Mexico. This led to the Alamo and the subsequent defeat of Santa Anna at San Jacinto, after which he was forced to sign a treaty recognizing Texas' independence. A decade later, after trying and failing to buy California and the New Mexico territory, the US started a war over that Mexican land. When people say they want to close the border with Mexico, they rarely consider that the border was originally one that we Americans illegally crossed.

Back in my native south, the abduction, enslavement, and ongoing forced relocation of Africans and their descendants shaped and was shaped by the land on this continent. Enslaved Africans were deemed necessary for the agriculture of the southern colonies and provided in ample supply by the Triangular Trade between Europe, Africa and the Americas. As the demand for cotton grew, Southern planters needed more land and more slaves to plant, tend, and pick the cotton. Manifest Destiny and the expansion of US territories in the West generated great contention over whether new states would allow slavery, eventually leading to the Civil War.

While some African Americans owned land in the early days of the United States, it was rare, and often subject to discriminatory zoning and other unjust policies. And after slavery, landholding remained tenuous and fraught with violence. Todd Lewan says that the desire for land motivated lynching and white mob attacks on blacks. The Associated Press documented 57 violent land takings in an 18-month investigation of black land loss in America. Sometimes, black landowners were attacked by whites simply out of hate. In other cases, the attackers did so in order to take the land for themselves.

Even the freedom to travel through our United States has been unequal based on racial discrimination and violence. African Americans depended on a Green Book to tell them what hotels, restaurants, and gas stations were safe to use while traveling during the rise in Interstate travel and the emergence of motels and roadside stops a plenty, for those who were white. Many towns in the US earned the label of "sundown towns," which indicated that African Americans found in the town after sundown would face forcible eviction or worse. Today, some areas in the US are still unsafe for travelers of color, a fact that is well-known among those affected but too often invisible to those of us unaffected.

With this history in our rear view mirror, it is challenging to stick with simple romantic images of the frontier and the open road. The lands we traversed in our van felt like home to us sometimes. That feeling sits alongside the reality of our history. It's complicated.

A Complex Love

After what I experienced on our trips, I began to ask myself: what does it mean to love a land beyond childish romance? What does a more mature, complex love for this land look and feel like?

I think it looks like listening to the people of the land. We can listen to the stories of the native peoples that ensured Lewis and Clark's survival during their explorations. We can find out about Old Toby, the Nez Perce, and Sakagawea who guided them on their journey, about the Mandan who provided food for their survival, about the Shoshone who provided horses for those places where boats couldn't traverse. We can learn about tribes and tribal lands in history and today. We honor their wisdom and traditions when we are willing to hear and tell the reality of pioneer and explorer stories.

Our van and American flag. Bear River State Park, Evanston, Wyoming

Is listening enough? It's a start. Ideally, listening is followed by action. It is easy to feel paralyzed by the weight of the injustices in our history. But when we let ourselves get stuck there, we forget that love is a verb. Like a long marriage, something Jim and I have experience with after 20 years together, real love is both persistent and compassionate.

Real love involves holding complex histories in the same heart as awe-inducing beauty and rich family and cultural traditions. Real love is grappling with the tension of doing family genealogy that involves land grants and slave censuses. Real love keeps its ears and heart open, even if that means some heartbreak along the way.

Nowadays, when I drive through America's wide open spaces, I can see beyond romantic images of pioneers and beyond simple images of American Indians as victims of displacement. I can see both the injustice and the bravery in the lives of settlers. I can admire the resilience and riches of Native American cultures while mourning what we all have lost through their displacement and genocide.

As the early American poet Walt Whitman wrote,

> The past and present wilt--I have fill'd them, emptied them,
> And proceed to fill my next fold of the future.
>
> Listener up there! what have you to confide to me?
> Look in my face while I snuff the sidle of evening,
> (Talk honestly, no one else hears you, and I stay only a minute longer.)
> Do I contradict myself?
> Very well then I contradict myself,
> (I am large, I contain multitudes.)

Travel brings us face to face with our past and present and offers the opportunity to forge a new future. My experience of the American west holds many contradictions, but like Whitman, I believe a mature love for our land is big enough to hold them all. Like the land itself, I can contain multitudes.

| 5 |

Lesson Five: Find Your Center

Rawlins, Wyoming, is the driest, windiest, dustiest place I've ever been. There's no place to eat except a steakhouse, a truck stop, and a combination KFC/Taco Bell. Crumbling motels line the main drag from one end of town to the other. As an aficionado of old roadside motels, I'm always on the lookout for these relics of an earlier travel age. I keep an eye out for that rare Thunderbird or cabin court, and am always tickled to find an old sign reading *Starlite* outside what are clearly now apartments for the down on their luck, or strange compounds with parking lots full of old VW Beetles and chickens walking around in the yard. The rare sight of well-kept-up older motels or cabin courts in small towns can bring me to a state of pure joy.

But I almost lost my love of old motels in Rawlins.

We came to Rawlins in the middle of our first cross-country van trip. On our way to Salt Lake City from our home outside Atlanta, we were five nights into our journey and already weary of the road because of moving camp every night to make it to Salt Lake in time for Jim's work.

I can work from anywhere, but was regretting the choice to work from the road after spending 6 hours the previous night in a truck-stop-adjacent campground rec room, hammering out a grant application, serenaded by big rigs pulling in and out and grumbling their engines all night.

I still had work to do to finish the document but was waiting for some items from a colleague that required a quick turnaround. I had no idea when they would come in. My back hurt. All our clothes were dirty. Truth be told, I wasn't in the best mood to begin with.

And then we got to Rawlins.

Before I go further in describing the most unredeemable spot on our trip, it might be helpful to know a little about Rawlins.

According to the official website of Rawlins, in 1867 a general and chief of staff of the US Army named John Rawlins was traveling this dry and desolate country and was desperate for "a drink of good, cold water." His men looked far and wide around the area and found a spring. Rawlins was so impressed by the water from this spring and asked that it be named after him, and so it was.

When your founding story is about someone desperately needing a drink of water while traveling through your area, I don't know if I would brag about that. I'm pretty sure Rawlins wished for that water because he had found the driest, windiest, dustiest place on earth. I never found the springs mentioned here, but they must have been refreshing; otherwise, I don't believe there would ever have been a community able to survive to bear the General's name.

Yet it does appear that such a community began in the late 1800s and continued on to today. Largely, this can be credited to the many pioneer trails that traveled through the area, and later the railroad, Lincoln Highway, and Interstate 80, the modern road that brought us to the area. The official website also notes some pleasant back roads and byways are in the area, but like the springs, I never found them. Perhaps my story of Rawlins would be very different if I had.

The Rawlins we experienced was one of dusty roads, aging motels, seedy bars, and empty storefronts.

It's funny — I typically love less photogenic places like swamps and deserts and Jim isn't bothered by anywhere with a good hike and wildlife. We loved more desolate scenery in the Badlands and in Teddy Roosevelt National Park, both in the Dakotas. We normally love post-boom small towns whose empty old storefronts have a certain ghost-town-adjacent charm.

So, what was the difference in Rawlins? Maybe it was the high winds that blew dust in our face the entire time we tried to set up camp. Or maybe it was the complete absence of quality food in town. We are easily pacified with a half decent takeout plate. Not this time.

Campsite, KOA, Rawlins, Wyoming

Even Poppy didn't want to be outside in the wind. She squinched her eyes closed against the dust whenever outside of the van. So we gave up and all clambered back inside. Fearing that our camping gear would be dirty beyond salvation, we kept most of it in the van, sleeping bent around it like a strange game of Tetris.

When camping in a minivan, it's rough to sit around in the van when it's not sleeping time. All of us, our gear, a foam mattress, and our drawers and camping potty all in a 4-8 space meant we each had approximately 4 inches per living being to enjoy. Every time we opened the doors, our bed and our mouths received a new dose of sandy dust. It's a miracle we fell asleep, but it's not like there was anything else to do in Rawlins.

And yet, when we woke up early the next morning to walk Poppy, a pronghorn deer was visiting our campsite as the sun rose over the buttes. Beauty was all around, even in Rawlins. All we had to do was wait for it to reveal itself.

I think the roots of my aggravation in Rawlins ran deeper than dust or dining woes. I have long struggled in the empty spaces of life. That seems counterintuitive when you think about how often we head from city life out into the much less crowded parts of our country.

But truthfully, the most well-known places in the American west are often some of the most crowded.

Colleen Creamer reported in the New York Times recently that 44 National Parks had more visitors in 2021 than in any previous year. A decade ago, when we went to Arches National Park in Moab, Utah, we felt stalked by the dozens of tour buses that showed up moments after we had arrived at each overlook. Almost as long ago, when we visited Yellowstone, there were times when the crowds felt as overwhelming as Disneyworld. And just a few months ago at Crater Lake National Park, we enjoyed relatively uncrowded overlooks, but the visitor center parking lot was full. We worried for a minute that we wouldn't be able to park for a bathroom break! Not exactly the experience of the lone traveler or couple gazing out across a majestic landscape in one of these American sacred places.

Road to Elkhorn Ranch Unit, Teddy Roosevelt National Park, Medora, North Dakota

Creamer's article highlights the lesser known and less crowded areas of popular national parks, for those seeking to avoid the crowds. We found one of those ourselves, quite unexpectedly. Teddy Roosevelt National Park, on the far western edge of North Dakota, is relatively crowded, with lines at the gate every time we came or went. We lucked out and got there in time to get one of the last campsites, though, so it's not like some that require reservations a year in advance. The visitor areas and overlooks were well visited but not crowded. However, we lucked out again when we found Elkhorn Ranch.

Almost an hour's drive from Medora, the village at the main park gate, Elkhorn Ranch Unit is where Teddy Roosevelt lived while grieving after his wife and mother died within hours of each other in 1884. After their deaths, he built the ranch and there retreated from political life for two years. As the NPS visitor guide emphasizes, Roosevelt built his ranch here "because of its remoteness." They don't exaggerate. It is in the middle of nowhere. A few fracking operations dot the landscape of high desert and butte badlands, but that's it. Our van shook side to side and up and down on the rough and rutted drive into the ranch. We lost cell signal miles before we reached the parking lot.

Tall weeds surrounded the lot. Our van was the sole vehicle in sight. We opened up the back doors, unloaded our camping chairs, and ate our ham sandwiches. Our rustling and the dogs whining for some ham were all we heard, other than the quiet whoosh of winds through the trees. After eating, a short walk over mowed but still brushy ground took us to the foundation stones of Roosevelt's old cabin. The soft winds and brilliant blue skies were our only companions. It was easy to see how this isolated, stark, and lovely place could be healing for Roosevelt in his time of grief.

Unlike the main Cottonwood campground, the campground out here was completely empty. It was open for the season. There just wasn't a soul there. Despite the natural beauty of the place, I couldn't imagine camping so far from anyone. Being so far out of cell range overnight was also unnerving.

Teddy Roosevelt National Park, Medora, North Dakota

We spent a few hours in the solitude before heading back to our campsite. Cooking our dinner 10 feet from the next campers cooking theirs and 30 feet from the bathhouse made us almost regret not camping out at Elkhorn Ranch. At least until that evening when I fell asleep happily watching TV on my phone.

Empty Spaces

The first spotting of one of my favorite corny jokes is thought to be in 1968, as graffiti on a warehouse wall. Here's how it was written:

> "The way to do is to be." -- Lao-tzu.
> "The way to be is to do." -- Dale Carnegie.
> "Do be, do be, do." -- Frank Sinatra.

I struggle with the idea of just being. Sitting in the metaphorical desert and listening to myself and to God is hard for me. Maybe that is why more desolate places like Rawlins can be hard for me to enjoy.

Doing -- I am the best at that. I am like the grand national champion of doing, many years running.

When trying new things, like planning our cross-country van trips, or starting our new publishing company, I normally get right to work. I frenetically research how to do it, and then start doing it posthaste. This approach works well for me, I get a lot done. Yet it can feel hectic and ungrounded at times.

The same is true for traveling. Faced with infinite choices about what roads to take and places to visit, great possibility lives alongside great vulnerability. Some call this vulnerability of uncertainty the spiritual desert, or the dark nights of the soul. We can avoid it if we stay busy enough planning and doing. But should we?

My tendency, of course, is to take in the vista of that desert for a few minutes, and then move on down the road. But I miss a lot when I skip over the empty places. When I can pull it off, staying in the empty places takes me deeper into my own heart and mind. I have to face and engage the uncertainty.

This requires a voluntary loss of control. A feeling that is not comfortable for me. At all.

I like to do things in the way that is required of me. To check the boxes, to meet the requirements, to plan my way out of any uncertainty. I like things locked down, all planned out, prepped in advance, and no surprises or unexpected detours. Unfortunately, or fortunately, as much as I tried to implement routines on our travels, I had to learn to hold plans loosely. I had to embrace the vulnerability of not knowing exactly what to do next.

Ernest Kurtz and Katherine Ketchum, who write on imperfection and spirituality, suggest:

> "Our ability to do, tends to outrun our be-ing. We love to manipulate, to bring about, to control--But our be-ing is more important, and there are some realities, realities essential to our very be-ing, that we cannot control. Indeed, the effort--the demand--to control them destroys not only them but ourselves."

There's a common thread through all of this. To travel is often to stop doing and controlling, and to give way to being and a loss of control. That's hard stuff. I can't out-do the being required to blaze new paths of imagination and experience.

In fact, I find I have to do a lot less to make space for new things to come into being. I struggle with this, because making plans is much more fun, and I see so much to do and fix in the world. Yet my soul is whispering — stay a second longer in the empty places. Step off the "do" train and just be on the platform for a while.

What a hard shift. As they say, what got you here might not get you there. Checklists, agendas, and lists of advice may need to be left behind to enter the empty spaces of the desert or wilderness. I am learning a new way, so I can go a new way.

Badlands National Park, South Dakota

Waiting

Sometimes, we don't have a choice about whether or not to wait. One day, Jim took Poppy for a hike in the Wasatch Range in Utah. I was driving and didn't realize there was no cell signal when we pulled into the trailhead parking lot. After we both took turns stepping into the restroom at the trailhead, Jim and Poppy took off up the hill toward the trail as I walked back to the van to rest. Altitude makes me sleepy, and I was looking forward to a nap.

I climbed into the back of the van and snuggled into the soft folding mattress, which in couch formation is the perfect size for me to get comfy. I pulled out my phone to play on social media before closing my eyes. Nope. No signal. Ok, fine, I decided, I'll just go straight into napping. But I couldn't settle down. I kept thinking about Jim in the woods. What if something happened, and he couldn't reach me? The simple fact of having no cell signal made it impossible for me to relax.

Ironic that we drive so many miles to get off the beaten path and here I couldn't take being off the grid. I decided to get busy cleaning and rearranging the van. Things get out of control fast living in such a small space, so there's always work to do there. Once that was done I thought it had been an hour or so, and so Jim would be back shortly.

I looked at the clock and it had only been 15 minutes. So I went up to the small ranger station next to the bathrooms and rifled through the selection of maps and books. That killed about 5 more minutes. I went back to the van and pulled out my Kindles. Both were dead. I cranked up the van to charge those and read through the pamphlet I had picked up at the ranger station. It had still been less than half an hour.

After about an hour of trying to entertain myself and distract myself from worries about Jim and Poppy out on the trail, having suffered numerous imaginary catastrophes with no way to reach me, I decided to hike up the trail toward them. I crossed the grassy field between the ranger station and the treeline, and as I neared the trailhead, Jim and Poppy appeared. Jubilation. All was well, and all my worries had been for naught.

It did make me think, though — when did I get so bad at waiting? Like empty places, open time can be stressful at first, a vacuum to be filled with activity. Yet part of finding our center involves learning to wait. Another new trail we must learn to navigate.

When my journey gets to a point where the map or cell signal runs out, or where moving isn't an option, and I have to get comfortable with the uncertainty of staying, sitting, and being, I turn to my faith.

One Bible text on waiting I love, at least partly because it contains a female religious prophet who bears my name. Simeon and Anna were known for their faithfulness. In Anna's case, she had been at the temple day after day for decades. Simeon waited year after year for a promised future he believed would save his people. They didn't try to do more to speed things up. At least not in this story.

And they didn't wait until they had done enough or until they had time to do it themselves to claim this dream of one who would bring healing and justice. They trusted in the everyday nature of God's promises and showed up to be in position for the dream to become reality. Day after day. Year after year. They showed up in the places they believed their God to be working. And in the place they believed God's promised future would someday arrive.

They probably felt lost at times, wondering if their long-awaited future would ever come. They knew where and how to show up, due to their religious tradition, but that doesn't mean it didn't seem uncertain and endless to them. Did they wonder if they would die before that day came? Did they doubt if they had heard God's calling and promise correctly? Did they grow weary of the wait?

Or did they find that waiting eventually settled into a quiet center, a place of communing with a God that is bigger than any empty place we can visit or imagine?

Finding myself on the open road meant finding my way into acceptance of uncertainty and empty places. I step onto paths that are unfamiliar but at the same time, profoundly familiar. I couldn't have walked this exact path 10 years ago, or 20, or 30. It took the wait for my location and next steps to be revealed.

Did Anna and Simeon find their years of waiting rich with realizations like that one? Rich with the gifts of the wait itself?

If you are anything like me, you can recognize theoretically that this waiting and being practice is right, a good and necessary thing, but still struggle with it. I'm restless. I'd rather do anything than spend time without my brain doing something. Checking something off my list, even a hated task, makes me happier than practicing stillness.

One thing I do, not as often as I should, is sit in front of a blank page and pour myself out, both to get lost and to be found. That's one way I practice facing the empty spaces at home. Or sometimes, like Simeon and Anna, I sit in my church to meet our creator, and to embrace all future possibilities. Other times, I sit in the driver's seat on a long road trip, willing to lose my certainty, my confidence, my illusions of control.

I still feel lost when I step up to a view, internal or external, of nothing but emptiness. I still doubt and wish for clarity about how well this life thing is going to go. Yet, when journeying across an empty dusty desert state, literally or metaphorically, in travel, in writing, or in other areas of life, I can look to Simeon and Anna, and remind myself to wait, trust, and just be.

Uncertain of the path ahead, but sure of God's faithfulness, I wait.

I am finally beginning to trust the wait. To trust the uncertainty as I am refined into a new creation. To trust that dusty winds can sandblast beauty out of rocky cliffs. To trust the benefits of this uncertain journey we call life, even in the empty places.

Finding the Center

People talk a lot about centering in terms of meditation and stillness, but it can be such a vague term. Center of what, exactly? We found one center on our journeys, but it also had issues of clarity.

Driving through the tiny town of Rugby, North Dakota, we caught a glimpse of an obelisk of stacked rocks in the middle of town. A plaque on the pyramid of stones read "Geographical Center of North America." The streets around the marker held a few businesses, a Subway here, a Family Dollar there. Powerlines and transmission towers loomed overhead. If this desolate little place is the center, what does that say about our great continent?

We had to stop at such a notable place, though. A windy drizzle pelted our faces as we got out of the car to look around. Not much to see. The obelisk was... well, an obelisk. Not even a very tall one.

In fact, Rugby may not actually be the geographical center of North America. Although the marker has been in Rugby since 1931, after someone balanced a map of the continent on a pin to see where it balanced, there is much debate about whether it is the true, real center. It may actually be in Robinson, ND, or Center, ND. Who knows? Or maybe the true center of North America is within us all, or the friends we make along the way, or something like that.

Geographical Center of North America Marker, Rugby, North Dakota

Finding our own centers, the inner place where we can wait and lean into being rather than doing, can feel much the same. We can't define it, or decide on what or where it is, so we live with a vague impression. There's no inner obelisk we can rely on for its location. It's up to each of us to find it on our own.

Traveling can be one way to search for this inner center. Simply because it can be so disorienting, travel often reveals to us the things within us that don't change. That place where we can balance all that we are on the head of a pin. Finding this center is often a challenge, but it's worth the trip.

One way I find my center on our travels is walking labyrinths.

Labyrinths originated in ancient times, but I was most familiar with their role in Christian history, as a substitute method of pilgrimage for those in the medieval era who could not travel to the Holy Land or to the place of a particular saint. The idea was that you would journey from the outside to the center and back again, symbolic of both a physical pilgrimage to another land and a spiritual deep dive into the inner self. A labyrinth is not a maze. There are no wrong turns or dead ends, and you will always walk the same route in that you will use to find your way out. Like visiting North America's geographical center, walking a labyrinth is much more about the journey than the destination.

Why would I take the time to seek out labyrinths while on an actual physical journey? I'm not sure. I think at first, I was seeking something familiar during what was otherwise a breakneck speed leg of our trip. Labyrinths provided an element of physically walking on new ground in these places that were new to us. Road trips, while way more ground-level than air travel, keep you gliding over the ground, separated by tires and the air under the vehicle. Since we often hit multiple states and/or landscapes in a day, going from mountain to prairie to mountain again, having my feet on the ground for the half hour it took to do a walking meditation/prayer in a labyrinth, meant something.

The simple labyrinth I found in Missouri was on the grounds of a small congregation. A weekday morning meant we were all alone with no one in sight as we parked. I took a few deep breaths and tried to focus on my movement along the path in and out of the circle of the labyrinth. There were a lot of distractions, and I keenly felt the pressure of needing to get it over with, so we could move along down the road. I still think it improved my mood and sense of centeredness, but certainly wasn't the Zen experience I had envisioned.

By my second road trip labyrinth, found in a park on the great plains in Nebraska, I had already gotten better at being fully present to an experience while also knowing there were more things on the agenda after that. Jim took Poppy for a walk while I walked, and it helped to not feel like someone was waiting on me. This labyrinth, in a public park, also felt less vulnerable to someone coming along who wondered what I was doing there, and where I would experience pressure to make conversation. No one expected anything of me or anyone else in this park.

I found my way into the labyrinth and out again. I walked it again. The third time, I took time to look at different elements, how it was constructed, where it was situated. I sat on a bench and just thought for a while.

By the third labyrinth, in the Cheyenne Botanical Gardens, I had gotten my routine down. I found my zen quicker than any of the others, and the natural setting brought a feeling of contentedness and peace.

These were not the only labyrinths along the way. But these three labyrinths across four days early in our van life framed and grounded things for all the days to come.

No matter how many literal or metaphorical miles you have ahead of you, it is always worth it to take time for a bit of waiting and being. A quiet center lives inside even when we are far outside our comfort zones. Labyrinths worked for me, but other practices might work for you. Take the time to figure out what they are and practice them, and your travel or life journey will be the better for it.

| 6 |

Lesson Six: Brake for Delight

Copper Harbor, Michigan is breathtakingly beautiful.

Lake Superior, Copper Harbor, Michigan

The expanse of Lake Superior fills the horizon. Charming little cottages and motels cluster in a tiny fishing village. The vibe is less tourist trap and more the Florida gulf coast oyster towns of my childhood. The state park campground on the edge of town was walkable to all of it, as well as a historic fort. We settled in happily in our little campsite and explored all morning.

Then the black flies came out.

We realized something was amiss when the spots where these small bugs landed on our arms and faces started dripping blood. Turns out, black flies literally cut your skin open and lick off the blood that comes out. These flies make mosquitos seem civilized. At least a mosquito keeps everything neat and tidy as it drains you of your blood.

From shortly after lunch until late at night, the black flies covered us. Bug spray didn't help. A fire we managed to start with our terrible fire starting skills only made a small dent in their number. Our screen house walls kept blowing sideways in the lake winds, letting them in by the droves.

We finally retreated into our van, hiding in there for hours with only a view of the bathhouse and other campers. We were merely steps away from a breathtaking landscape and couldn't enjoy it. Sometimes life on the road just sucks.

When you travel for weeks at a time, there are actually a lot of things that aren't that great. Your laundry bag gets fuller and smellier as you search in town after town for a decent laundromat. You end up buying leggings at a Dollar General more than once after your clean clothes run out. When you finally find a tiny laundromat, you have flashbacks to college as you wait impatiently for people to get their gosh-darn clothes out of the dryer so you can start yours.

The campsite you were so tickled to get in a National Park has no electricity. You are out of butane and propane. You try to cook in the rice cooker with it plugged in to the running van, but it flips the surge protector every minute and a half. You go to town to find all the restaurants crowded and so get some bison summer sausage at the convenience store. You are so hungry by the time you get back to the campsite, you eat standing up, cutting off slices with a dull knife. You have an upset stomach for days.

Experiences like that can make you want to head straight home, with haste.

What keeps you going is delight.

Roadside Respites

Sometimes delight surprises you along the way. Sometimes you have to make your own. A road trip game I like to play is spotting old motels. Something about their low-slung profile, arranged around the parking lot or pool, all the doors lined up side by side, makes me smile. Whether still in operation, converted to apartments, or falling down in disrepair, they speak to me of road trips past, mostly before my time. As a kid, I got to stay in a few charming old beach motels on summer trips, the kind with doors that opened right on the pool deck, only a few short steps to the ocean. I swam from the time I woke up until my parents made me get out of the water and go to bed. It was heaven.

I also remember one or two not so heavenly motels on trips where my parents could find no other lodging. Those were the days you might find numerous "no vacancy" neon signs in crowded vacation destinations, long before online booking was even a concept. These occasional unwanted forays into old motels left a lot to be desired, particularly in terms of cleanliness. The reality of old motels is unreliable, at best.

The romantic ideal of motels in my imagination, however, is dreamy and nostalgic for a past I barely experienced. In my imaginary trips back in time to roadsides of the mid-20th-century, old motels played a huge role. A Brady Bunch type family could take a trip from the east coast all the way to Disneyland or the Grand Canyon, staying in motor courts every night along the way. Postcards and old movies show roadside motels as everything from romantic to horrific, with a definite lean toward the noir. A detective or someone on the run might hole up in one off the beaten path, blinking neon lighting their window through the night. And of course, a disturbed young man could terrorize a young woman in a shower one scary night.

On our trips, I have us take the old roads where you are most likely to find such classic motels. Each one I spot casts new stories on the screen of my mind. I'm sure Jim loves my constant exclamations when I spot one.

At Fort Bridger, the Wyoming Department of State Parks and Cultural Resources has restored the buildings of one of the earliest motor courts on the Lincoln Highway. Little more than a shell of a building now, it still conjured images of those earliest road trippers from the 20s and 30s finding a haven here, in a room with a garage attached for your car.

Carla's Motel, Baraga, Michigan

It brought to mind a travel show that featured the ruins of cave lodgings for caravans in the desert. These multi-chamber caves had room for animals to be stabled next to a covered place to bed down for the night. There were even vendors serving dinner in the common areas. Not that different from a Howard Johnson!

We still wander, we still seek food and lodging, more through apps these days than in caves or along neon-lit roadsides. What adventures can we find if we step away from the standardization of national chains into the historic havens of prior generations on the road? It can be a mixed bag, for sure. But I think it's worth the trouble to find out.

On our way south from the Great Lakes, we needed a break from the van. I searched for dog friendly lodging along our route and found a motel in Saginaw, Michigan. The name Saginaw holds a romance for me since the day I first heard it in Simon and Garfunkel's song America. The small city didn't live up to that romance, but was pretty typical for the north Midwest. Its downtown was rich with historic buildings but emptied out on a weekday evening. There was a post-industrial vibe.

After taking a look around the city, I programmed the motel address into my phone's GPS. It was further from town than I realized, but figured it must be along a major highway or thoroughfare. Wrong. The phone directed us south out of town on Highway 13. Five lanes narrowed to four, then three, then two. Businesses gave way to little frame houses that stretched further apart the farther we drove. Houses gave way to fields. We couldn't imagine a motel out here, among the farmland. But we persisted, figuring that if the motel didn't work out, we were still heading south toward home.

After miles of this scenic if sparsely populated drive, we saw in the middle of a field a most unexpected site. There it was. The Relax Inn. A small brown sign with yellow writing told us it was the right place. The low slung U of three one story buildings had all the characteristics of a historic roadside motel. We turned left into the parking lot and rolled up in front of the red door marked simply, Office. A soda machine sat by the door so we knew we could at least find refreshment of some sort here.

The office smelled a little off, maybe of old cigarette smoke. There was a language barrier with the clerk when confirming that our dog was welcome as well. Once checked in, we found that the room itself was so small that the door brushed the back of one of the dining chairs at the table by the window. The adjoining bathroom — well, if you forgot to shut the door before you sat down it wouldn't clear your knees to do so after. Tiny coffee maker, tiny microwave, and tiny fridge made up the kitchenette next to the oversized TV armoire. Yet the decor was updated and the room was clean, spotless even, cleaner than many rooms we've had at much higher end lodgings. Ordinary, but done with excellence.

The sublime, though, was walking out of the room and around the back of the motel. Our building backed up to a field of waving corn. Cornflower blue overhead, dotted with luminous clouds, took our breath away. The only sounds were the breeze rustling the stalks and the occasional car going by on the two-lane. Delight was there for the taking, even in an old motel on a two-lane country road outside Saginaw, Michigan.

Other favorite architecture seen on our journey was in the most unlikely of places. While we took the time where we could to seek out notable structures by Frank Lloyd Wright and others, some of the most striking architecture sat right on the side of the road.

Rest areas evolved as the highways did. Travelers needed a spot to find a bathroom and grab refreshments, and every so many miles, the highway systems or local municipalities soon provided roadside parks at no charge. The 1956 Federal Aid Highway Act launched the funding and development for interstate highways across the country. While towns were often excited about the interstate highways coming near, over the years, the way the highways flew past, not through the downtowns, dooming many to become declining or ghost towns today.

Some towns, though, invested in their rest areas. Many showcased local flair such as windmills, oil-rig shaped structures, or statues and murals for photo opportunities. Others featured more exploitative architecture, such as structures meant to evoke the habitations of Native Americans. These unique designs reminded travelers that they were in a real place, not just another generic stretch of miles that looked much like the last. Rest areas were later federally funded and seen as public assets, ambassadors for the modernity and quality of their state.

Much of this rest stop architecture remains the same today as when originally developed in the mid-20th century. We found sweeping V covered picnic tables in Nebraska, tepee shapes further west, and mid-century modern breeze-block surrounds that helpfully broke the plains winds as we ate our sandwiches.

I think of all the rest areas I took for granted over the years. They may seem terribly ordinary, but for a weary traveler, space to take a break amid some uplifting architecture can make all the difference in the world.

Cows and Other Critters

Between old motels and rest areas on the open highway, you have a lot of time to think. And look for cows.

When I was a kid, my family would often listen to Garrison Keillor's Prairie Home Companion on our area's public radio station on Sunday afternoons. We had a cassette tape full of particularly good songs and stories, so we could listen outside of the scheduled live show every week. This was way before any kind of streaming on demand. If you didn't catch it on the radio, buying a tape, often in exchange for a pledge to public radio, was the only option for repeated listening.

I don't remember a lot of the skits, but one that I never forgot and is much referenced in my family, involves a young man named Johnny Tollefson heading for college, riding in the car with his family. He is mortified by his family's continual comments on the billboards and animals they spot along the way. This is contrasted with a much more urbane family from books he loves — the Flambeaus, a family that leads elegant lives in New York City while solving crimes. So many times, my mother and I referenced the Tollefson Boy story, which echoed our own rural natures that contrasted with our literary and academic interests. We would nickname someone fancy the Flambeaus. We would call out in mock Midwestern accents on road trips, reading every billboard or announcing every animal we spotted in a field along the way, just like Johnny's mortifying relatives.

We had two close cow encounters out in the Midwest, the originating land of Keillor's prairie stories. On a teeny tiny road in Iowa, we pulled over to the side to check the directions. I sensed a movement to my right and glanced up and out of the car window. To my surprise and delight, a number of cows have come up to the fence and are looking at us with what appears to be an inquisitive curiosity in their soft, gigantic eyes. While I have seen many cows at a distance, it is a rare occasion to be eyeball to eyeball, a couple feet apart like this. My heart grows three sizes as they gaze at me. I want to hug them. Somehow, we tore ourselves away and moved on down the road. I wonder what the cows thought of this encounter. I am still thinking about it years later.

Along another fence line at the Ingalls Homestead in South Dakota, a family in the camper next to ours asked us to join them for a birthday party. They had brought out a cake, and we all sang to their daughter in honor of her special day. What a treat that would have been for me as a little girl, to celebrate a birthday in the land of these beloved books, and I was so proud to be a part of it for another young fan. As we sang, something again caught my eye off to the side. Across the road from our party was a barbed wire fence. A group of cows eased closer and closer to the fence until, during our song-ending applause, they had gathered right up against the fence. After enjoying our cake, we took the dogs over to investigate. I couldn't help but wonder — what did the cows think about attending the birthday party?

Cows, Ingalls Homestead, De Smet, South Dakota

It has gotten less of a comedy routine and more of a reality over time. I have now fully become a middle-aged lady drawing attention to every set of cows I discover along the roadsides. It feels important for some reason to exclaim, "Cows!" wherever I see them. I can't explain it. But I also can't escape it.

Such encounters are the everyday stuff of road trips. They are also points of delight, connection, and feeling grounded in a particular place. Don't worry about being the rubes who stop and look at cows. After all, they took the time to come over and look at you, so a little reciprocation is only polite.

Cows are great but not our favorite road-trip critters. Those tiny friends, seen often in Teddy Roosevelt National Park and at stops along I-80, were the prairie dogs.

Not a cow, but we saw plenty of bison too!

We saw our first prairie dog at the Little America truck stop in Little America, Wyoming. Yes, the town is named after the truck stop. The Little America is part of a company known as the Grand America Hotels and Resorts, and Jim stayed at the very grand Grand America hotel in Salt Lake City a few years back. The Littles are less grand, but still notable in their own right. This Little America in Wyoming was the first motel the company ever built, first along the old Lincoln Highway and now along I-80. Starting as a simple roadside motel, it expanded to become the world's largest filling station for many years running. That was reason enough for me to stop.

The truck stop was just a truck stop, though, nothing too remarkable, and the dog park was made of so many rocks that Poppy kept looking back at me as if to ask, is this a joke? The real treat was right in front of our van, in the green and dirt median between us and the access road. As I walked Poppy back to the van, something was moving in the grass near our front bumper. My brain couldn't make sense of it at first. Getting closer, it looked like a real life version of whack-a-mole. I realized I was seeing something I'd only ever heard about — prairie dogs!

They popped up and glanced our way over and over, making it clear they had their eyes on us, and we should be on our best behavior. We saw them again in Teddy Roosevelt National Park, which has a whole field of prairie dog burrows, with a trail in the middle of the field for easy viewing of the show. These twitchy critters again eyed us with suspicion. I'm sure if Poppy and Pepper weren't kept on a leash at all times, the little creatures' caution would be well warranted!

No dogs allowed in the inner part of the field, though. For the prairie dogs' sake.

Teddy Roosevelt National Park, Medora, North Dakota

A Game for Your Next Road Trip: Churches v. Bars

Spotting cows, motels or prairie dogs were fun games, and we soon added another to our road trip repertoire. Before we headed west across the US, a friend challenged us to play a game called Churches vs. Bars. Simply put, while traveling you count the number of each in a town and figure out whether that town is a Bar town or a Church town. We soon noticed that as we got past the Mississippi and even more so past the plains, bars began to win much more consistently than churches. The gap grew and grew until

> we couldn't remember the last town where churches won. Then at the end of our trips, as we traveled south from the Great Lakes, the reverse occurred. Slowly but surely, churches outnumbered bars, and we knew we were on our way home to the church-heavy deep south of our native Georgia.

Roadside Rhythms

Delight often came with a melody. In addition to our daily singalongs when a favorite song came on the radio, our ramble through the southeast toward points west was rich with musical connections.

Mural, West Memphis, Arkansas

In Dyess Colony, Arkansas, hometown of Johnny Cash, we learned how the whole community was an agricultural settlement project of the New Deal. Meant to take people from subsistence farming, often as sharecroppers owing their soul to the company store, to a more settled and agribusiness lifestyle. New residents (whites only) received a plot of land with a house and livestock in an area with rich Mississippi Delta soil. The idea was that the community would be cooperatively owned and coordinated, self-supporting, and provide all it needed for its residents, while the settlers would work over time toward paying back obligations and earning full ownership of their land. The idea of founding a community to help people move from struggle to stability is appealing. Unfortunately, a lot of the territory was swampy, and farming is hard work in the best of conditions, so life was still not easy for the farming families seeking a new start in Dyess. Johnny and his brother grew up here, until a farming accident took his brother's life, breaking the family in ways that shaped the boy who would later become The Man in Black.

Johnny Cash Boyhood Home, Dyess, Arkansas

The little town where residents would shop, visit, and worship was hardly there anymore, but we walked around a few storefronts, and went in one which had been made into a museum about life in Dyess. The Cash home has been also preserved as a historical site, but only for scheduled tours, so we only glimpsed the outside of that simple white frame dwelling from the road. In Dyess, the challenges of life during the depression shaped those like Cash, who would later shape American pop culture.

A similar humble homestead in Tupelo was preserved as the birthplace of Elvis Presley. Another poor farm boy who lost a brother too young (Elvis' twin died at birth), his family was forced to move along when he was only a few years old due to financial hardship. The birthplace park provides a glimpse into rural life for poor whites in the south, with the humble shotgun home where he lived as a small child and the Presley's family church, which was later moved to the site. Across the road, we walked a trail back through the woods to a swimming hole. Our dogs liked the walk, although it was too buggy for us to enjoy. From the creek bank, you could almost picture Elvis and other kids swinging out on a rope and making a big splash to cool off on a muggy hot morning many years ago.

Further west, next to the old Walnut Ridge, Arkansas depot, a Guitar Walk featured some rockabilly stars with less name recognition than Elvis. This guitar-shaped path contains markers every few feet that provide information on various early rockabilly stars. Bridging hillbilly music, blues, and the beginnings of rock and roll, rockabilly was wild and flamboyant, an influence on Elvis, the Beatles, and other rockers that came along in later years. Well-known names like Johnny and Elvis were honored alongside lesser-known artists such as Wanda Jackson and Sonny Burgess. Each marker would bring the musician to life by playing one of their performances at the push of a button.

Walnut Ridge was doubly musical, with a life-size metal silhouette of the Beatles just a few blocks away, in honor of a brief visit the band made after landing at an airport there en route to a nearby farm for hunting and recreation. The town remembers this brief visit so many years ago in a small concrete park between downtown buildings. A sculptural silhouette of the Fab Four is perfect for photo ops if you can find the place. However, the concrete keeps it from being a park where one would linger.

Guitar Walk, Walnut Grove, Arkansas

Small towns must make the most of what they can to draw outsiders for tourism and spending money. Walnut Ridge seized on their musical connections in a way that got us to swing by, so it's working!

Downtown Walnut Grove, Arkansas

Mountain View, AR, spotlighted a different musical genre. The Ozark Folk Center presents old time music and folk craft exhibits on a dog-friendly outdoor campus. A parking lot down at the bottom of the hill offers shuttles up to the exhibits, but with the dogs, we chose to make the climb up the hill path instead. Finding our way into the exhibit area was challenging, as the only way in was through a building that didn't appear to be a place for dogs, but after that initial hallway, an open courtyard made for a pleasant afternoon sitting with dogs, listening to some bluegrass picking-and-grinning. We took turns visiting the interior of the craft areas where dogs would be less welcome. Seeing weaving and spinning, candle dipping, and instrument crafting was a bonus, but the true highlight was the musical performances. Every half hour or so another musician or ensemble would take the covered stage, visible from the courtyard, and spin songs and tales to bring the folkways of the region to vivid life. We weren't picking, but we were definitely grinning at these musical delights.

Zooming In

From the level of a US map, or a state one, you can't zoom in enough to see delight. A trip looks mechanical, simply getting from place, to place, to place. There's no way to capture how the smallest moments of a trip grant the most joy.

Like in SuperTown. Metropolis, IL, is synonymous with Superman. A giant statue of the superhero in the middle of town serves as both roadside attraction and photo backdrop. Of course, we had to take our turn getting a picture with the man of steel. Shops feature tons of Superman merchandise and Man of Steel fans can find anything of interest in one of them. Other than Superman though, the town had the weekday emptiness of most small towns we passed through. Foot traffic was limited to the superfans stopping to visit the big man. While tourism can bring people to a small town, it can't make it lively without other changes that engage the locals, and in Metropolis, locals were thin on the ground. Of course, it could have been that too many battles between Superman and bad guys over the years had taught people to keep inside and out of the fray. That's more fun to imagine, anyway.

And in stormy Mackinaw City, Michigan. The rain and fog was so thick we couldn't even get a good view of the big bridge or great lakes. Jim's paddle board tour of the lake shore was cancelled. At a loss for what to do with our day, we stopped at a local pasty shop. These baked meat hand pies overflowed with beef, onions, gravy, and, to Anna's delight, rutabaga (called swedes here in the Upper Peninsula). That night we had locally grown wild rice and locally smoked salmon cooked in our rice cooker. This waterlogged and unscenic day of our trip was one of the most delicious.

Or in Renfro Valley, KY. When we stopped for the night at a small KOA perched on a hill above the town, we soon found out that Renfro Valley is a historic homeland of country music. The Renfro Valley Barn Dance has taken place continuously since 1939, and for many years, was broadcast over the radio, similar to the Grand Old Opry. Another radio show, The Renfro Valley Gatherin' is the second longest continually broadcast country music show on the radio after the Opry. Now, also home to the Kentucky Music Hall of Fame and Museum, there is no shortage of attractions here for music lovers.

All this radio history was great, but the real treasure sat on the same hilltop as the KOA, across the parking lot in a small beige building marked WRVK. As longtime fans of quirky local radio, of course we had to find it on our car radio as we drove to pick up some dinner. We were delighted to hear Pete Stamper, WRVK DJ (and notable singer/songwriter in his own right) reading the local classifieds on a show called, "Whatcha Got?" Imagine hearing your Facebook Marketplace ad read aloud to the whole community. "Sheila Edgar has a metal table with 1 medium dent for sale. 30 dollars. Call 227-555-1122" "Carl has a room for rent with shared bathroom, email him for more information at carl@gmail.com." "Free. Four female small pigs, potbelly. Call 227-555-3344." You get the picture. It was adorable.

Pete Stamper died in 2020, so there's no revisiting that experience. You can never step into the same river twice. The fleeting nature of places and people we encounter on the road is its own kind of miracle.

Finding delight wherever we could changed our experience of the road. Animal sightings, silly road games and everything in between lifted us beyond the stress and worry of daily #vanlife. Remembering that lesson for when life off the road gets stressful — delightful!

Cow! At Ingalls Homestead, De Smet, South Dakota

| 7 |

Lesson Seven: Lose Your Place

Jim steered the van into the correct lane at the Canadian border, putting the van in park next to the guard station. We were about to cross our first international border together.

I was a sleepless nervous wreck the night before. I read over and over the rules and regulations for border crossings. I triple-checked that I had all the information needed for us and our dogs. But as we got closer to the border, camping first in North Dakota, then in the International Peace Garden right at the border, my anxious mind fixated on the wide variety of things we had in our van for camping, from butane to bear spray to knives, and so on. Sitting in the van and waiting for the border guard to come to the window and tell us what to do, my heart beat fast and my breath came shallow.

I'm normally an anxious person, but this was a bit much even for me. Why was I so scared of this first trip through a border checkpoint?

Unfamiliarity was certainly a factor. Jim had never been outside the country. My one foray out of the continental USA was to Tijuana for a single afternoon, back when a driver's license would suffice to cross, well before 9/11. Riding in the back seat with San Diego locals who knew the process well, the border barely made an impression. We were not exactly seasoned international travelers.

Also, the general atmosphere of the U.S. in recent years has kept migration on my mind. Canada seems like the most likely option if my family had to immigrate. Canada often seems Utopian to me, with their public health care and reasonable gun laws. Easy to say when you don't live there, I guess. But when our national news is featuring science denial and racist mobs, Canada does seem above the fray. Their socialized medicine would be a massive relief for us personally, since private health insurance and the American health care system take a good chunk of our paychecks and at least some time every week handling billing errors and appeals for the most basic of care. Plus Canadians just seem really nice.

I have said many times that we should move to Canada, half-jokingly in my younger years and then increasingly less jokingly as we got older. But the idea that we could move to another country felt like mere fantasy. In spite of having a few friends who moved away to live the expat life abroad, it still seemed like one of those things only other people do. Border issues becoming a hot political issue and constantly on the news didn't help. If our country became unwelcoming to all immigrants, would other countries reciprocate accordingly? If we did need to migrate away from the US someday, would we be able to do so?

A few years back, when things in our country started getting slightly intense politically, we applied for our passports. Jim had one a long time ago that expired without getting a single stamp, and I had never had one at all. The few people we told asked what kind of trip we were planning. It was a little awkward to admit we didn't have any immediate international travel plans. The expense and trouble are not unsubstantial to take this mostly symbolic gesture. But I wanted to make sure we could leave, if it ever came down to it.

Sitting at the border station, I thought through how I had packed the van in the campground strategically. I had checked on every item which could be slightly questionable, placing them on top and easy to get to in case the border patrol asked to check them.

But the border guards didn't look at one bit of my careful organization. The border patrol did ask us to come into a small waiting room while they ran our passports, but they didn't check the van, the dogs, or even the dogs' papers! It turned out to be relatively painless, and as usual the amount of time I spent worrying was way worse than the situation itself. I'm sure most Americans and Canadians do these kinds of crossings without any concern at all.

Afterwards, we pulled over for a photo at the sign saying Welcome to Canada. Stepping foot on foreign soil for the second time in my life felt like a giant exhale. Relief that my worry over the crossing was over joined thankfulness for the ability to travel freely across borders. I will never take that freedom lightly in these troubled times.

Welcome Sign, Manitoba, Canada

Those Who Cross

Like rivers, borders and their crossings seemed ever-present on our travels.

After grabbing a pizza in the first town north of the Canadian border, we drove for miles along perfectly straight roads with wheat fields stretching across the horizon. We finally saw in the distance an intersection with a cluster of houses and barns. The sign said Neubergthal. We had arrived.

I had reserved a historic cottage that was once home to the community herder for the Mennonite village of Neubergthal, Manitoba, and now part of a National Historic Site. We needed a break from the van, and sleeping in a real historic site seemed too good to pass up. A quick survey revealed several buildings in crisp white and red, with broad tin roofs that rose steeply up at least three stories high. Mixed with the historic structures were modern ranches and bungalows. This historic site was still a living community, and we got to live in it. For a few days, anyway.

Pulling into the circular gravel drive in front of one of the largest of the barn-like structures, our hosts, Margruite and Paul Krahn greeted us. Margruite and Paul have family connections to the original Mennonites who settled this area. They showed us to our home for a few days, set back from the road up against yet another wheat field.

The tiny white cottage with green trim held three main rooms, with a tiny kitchen and bath added off the side at some point for more modern conveniences. An outhouse still stood at the back corner of the yard demonstrating that less modern conveniences were a reality here as well. Stepping inside, the brightly painted floors and whitewashed walls lifted our road-weary hearts.

Herdsman's Hut, Neubergthal, Manitoba

This little cottage had once been a herdsman's hut. Such a herdsman would serve the whole community by taking everyone's animals out to the communal pastures and back. For an agricultural community like Neubergthal, he was definitely an essential employee. The herder's home was filled with historic but comfortable furniture. Everything was eminently practical, but there was a touch of whimsy in the colorful patterns on the floors. Turns out, floor painting was a traditional folk art of the Canadian Mennonites. The women would work on their art during the winter when the farms were dormant and farm chores were less all-consuming. They brought unique patterns and motifs to this work, using rags, corncobs and other things found around the farm to bring them to life. Our host, Marguerite, is herself an artist who has dedicated part of her work to preserving and recreating this folk art.

Schlafenbank and Painted Floor, Herdsman's Hut, Neubergthal, Manitoba

One of the beds was a Schlafenbank, or sleeping bench, a transforming piece of furniture unique to Mennonites, particularly those who immigrated to the Canadian prairie. Having Schlafenbanks allowed more seating during the day and more sleeping when needed at night.

The kitchen and bathroom were basic, with an old farmhouse sink and claw foot tub. The toilet was the composting variety. Historic structures don't have a lot of flexibility for adding modern plumbing. Technology is another modern convenience that was intentionally left out of the herdsman's hut. There was no TV to disrupt the prairie peace.

The heart of the house was a fireplace used for heating and cooking. Its stocky white plaster column opened to the living room and both bedrooms with oven compartments for baking. Inside the column were maze-like passages so that the smoke could heat every brick in the column before venting out the top. The thick brick walls of the fireplace would hold heat overnight, perfect for use in cold climates like Manitoba. These fireplaces are known as Russian stoves and are common in historic homes in Russia, Ukraine, and Belarus.

Who are these people that brought traditions like community herders, floor painting, German Schlafenbanks and Russian stoves to their new homes in Canada?

Our hosts told us all about them. A group of radical Anabaptists were persecuted in Holland and Switzerland during the Protestant Reformation. They became known as Mennonites because they followed the teachings of a priest named Menno, and left those countries for lands now in Poland. Here they found welcome and began to develop a unique culture set apart by their faith and their German language. Eventually, though, that welcome cooled, and they were shut out of land purchases there. They then moved to the steppes of southern Russia where they had been offered welcome. One of the colonies formed there was called

Russian Fireplace and Painted Floor, Herdsman's Hut, Neubergthal, Manitoba

Bergthal. Soon enough, Russian policies and restrictions influenced them to seek yet another area to practice their faith and culture.

It was then that some of these Mennonites moved to Canada, and formed the little community called Neubergthal (literally, new Bergthal). Others ended up in different areas of North America, spreading in wave after wave across Canada and the USA and southward into Mexico and other parts of Latin America.

Neubergthal is significant in that the preserved buildings reflect both the culture these immigrants had brought with them and adaptations they made to the climate and land in this new place. Margruite also gave us tours of a historically preserved hausbarn and the converted barn she and her husband call home as well as artist's studio and event space. Hausbarns are a house and barn combined, with living quarters in the front and animal quarters in the back, so that the warmth of the animals helped heat the houses and the farmers did not have to go out in driving or deep snow to tend to their stock. Another clever adaptation to their new homes.

It was hard to leave Neubergthal and the peaceful quiet of unplugged life on the prairie. But the road was calling, and it was time to go.

Living inside the immigrant past in Neubergthal gave us a sense of being grounded and connected to this land ourselves. Yet, as our hosts acknowledged, this land was taken from the indigenous Anishinaabe and Swampy Cree through unjust and unfulfilled treaties only shortly before the Mennonites arrived.

Our immigrant experiences along our journey didn't start or end with our Canadian Mennonite friends.

In North Dakota, we visited parks with historic buildings honoring Scandinavian, Czech, and German immigrants, with Stave churches, Finnish saunas, and a statue of Hans Christian Anderson.

Stave Church, Scandinavian Heritage Park, Minot, North Dakota

In Michigan, we visited a town so full of immigrants during its mining heyday, it had not only churches of every denomination but six Catholic churches to serve all the different languages and cultures recruited from abroad to immigrate and work in mines. We also crossed in and out of numerous tribal nations and learned about the movements of these peoples before they were forced on reservations by the evils of manifest destiny.

One group of people's land of freedom and plenty is often the same land where other groups have been forcibly displaced. Border crossings for those fleeing persecutions are also often border crossings which yield personal gain at the expense of another. No border story is a simple story.

In the Bible, there is a terrible story of Mary, Joseph, and Jesus fleeing because Herod is trying to kill all children under two in and around Bethlehem. The text references an earlier passage about a mother weeping for her lost children with loud lamentation and wailing, refusing to be consoled, because they are no more.

This genocide was committed because Herod believed Jesus was a threat to his rule and had to be found and eliminated. Although Jesus and his family were already in Egypt, Herod believed that by killing all the children in Bethlehem, he would no longer have to worry about a usurper to his throne.

Herod's murderous acts recall other Biblical acts of genocide: The text from Jeremiah regarding a weeping mother is set during the destruction of Jerusalem by the Babylonians, who exiled members of prominent Israelite families to foreign lands. Keeping the workers behind to do their bidding. And of course, the Herod story mirrors the tale of Pharaoh killing firstborn babies in the time of Moses' birth. In all of these slaughters, a ruler is threatened by the potential of an oppressed people to rise up and overthrow his rule.

Stories are also told of those rulers failing at their objectives. The Israelites persist as a people and culture despite slavery and exile. Jesus' reformation of loving neighbor over law persists even after his death. However, we can't forget that in spite of these reversals of fortune, babies died. Families were separated. People had to leave the only homes they had ever known. We forget too how Mary and Joseph must have lost nieces and nephews, and the children of their friends.

Like the Mennonites, they had to cross borders and leave behind much that they loved to keep their families safe and sound.

Without Borders

Is there such a thing as a world without borders? In the two days before we crossed the Canadian border, we visited and camped at the International Peace Garden. The Peace Garden is a place without a country, by intention. By treaty, it is neither part of the US or part of Canada, although lands from both countries were given to make up the park. The international border runs directly along the midpoint of the park, surrounded by lush plantings and trees. This is a place dedicated to peace in nature and peace between nations.

International Peace Garden, Boissevain, Manitoba

The International Peace Garden began as an idea in the mind of Dr. Henry J. Moore, an Ontario doctor who dreamed of a border garden where people could connect and celebrate international friendships. His idea became a project of the National Association of Gardeners, who chose a site along the Canadian border, near the geographical center of North America, in 1932. The land was donated by the

Canadian province of Manitoba and the US state of North Dakota. Thousands attended ceremonies for the groundbreaking and dedication. Over 2000 acres was dedicated to this garden project, which now includes wooded trails, formal botanical gardens, demonstration plots, interpretive centers, a museum, a chapel, a 9/11 memorial, event and camping facilities, and more.

During the many wars following its founding, the Peace Garden served as an inspiration for and reminder of the value of peace. While others were endorsing fascism and concentration camps abroad, endorsing isolationism, or interning Germans and Japanese here in the "land of the free," there were people dedicated to building peace in their own small way.

Campsite, International Peace Garden, Boissevain, Manitoba

In the heart of the Peace Garden is the Peace Chapel. Made of stone and colored glass panels, the mid-century modern sanctuary was built in 1968. The Manitoba limestone walls are etched with quotes of peace from international leaders. Alone in the space, I walked the walls slowly and read each of the peace quotes etched in the walls in turn. I sat on one of the benches and tried to think of a hymn I knew well enough to sing without music. The closest I got was Come Thou Fount of Every Blessing. When I got to "I hope, by thy good pleasure, safely to arrive at home," I realized I had selected the perfect traveler's hymn.

This was not the only Peace Garden we encountered on our travels. In Salt Lake City, the International Peace Gardens along the banks of the Jordan River became a favorite spot for walks with our dog, Poppy. She loved the many paths to explore and smell while I was drawn to the unique architecture and design of the garden. Like the International Peace Garden on the Canadian border, the idea for this garden came to Mrs. Otto Ruey Wiesley before World War II. Organized by the Salt Lake Council of Women with local parks departments and dedicated in 1952, the gardens represent 28 ethnic groups and nationalities, with different beds or areas of the garden inspired by those cultures. There are pagodas, sculptures, Greco-Roman columns, obelisks, a mini-Eiffel tower, and much more, all surrounded with plantings representing the colors or native plants of the corresponding countries.

In these gardens, it was easy to imagine all countries living in harmony when their gardens adjoin each other happily and moving from one to the other is as easy as taking a few steps.

Our border experiences opened my eyes to a new awareness. For most of my life, I thought of immigrants and refugees as others. Forced migration or immigration for a better life was something that happened to other people. Now I see that we are not so different after all. Hard life conditions like war or persecution can happen to anyone. Any one of us may need the welcome of another land someday. Part of our work in the world is making sure our land is welcoming. It's a pretty big part of loving your neighbor and doing unto others as you would have them do unto you.

In the meantime, while we do this work, it benefits each of us to cross a border occasionally. Or at least learn about those who crossed borders in our national story. Those experiences open our eyes, so we can see the gifts given by and given to those who cross.

| 8 |

Lesson Eight: Stay Rooted and Keep Branching

We drove up Main Street somewhere in middle America and parked in one of the angled spaces facing the shop fronts. Well, only a few were actually shops. Most were offices or for rent. The windowed front of a discount women's clothing retailer featured mannequins in various states of undress. It was not clear if this was business as usual or if they were in the middle of a refresh. This railroad town had no square, just this strip of shops and the railroad tracks across the street. The wood sign in front of a tired little gazebo on a lot of grass read Civitan Park. Honestly, I can't remember the name of that town or what state we were in. I do remember that my imagination took over, like it does in every small town. What if I rented that space and opened a book store? If I lived here, would I walk downtown to shop or get some exercise? What would it be like to reserve the park gazebo for a birthday party? Could I be happy here?

I don't know why small towns make me so reflective. Especially since I spent most of my first 30 years plotting how to get out of them.

Born in a Small Town

I grew up in Moultrie, a small town in southwest Georgia, and spent my early married years in an even smaller one. Most of the time, I wanted nothing more than to leave those places behind and never look back. As soon as I could, I moved to bigger communities, and I am still happily settled in metro Atlanta to this day.

Small towns that are not my hometown hold a fascination for me though. Daydreams capture my attention in every little town we pass through. My mind comes alive dreaming about what life could be like there. I mourn the ghostly empty downtowns of those that time left behind. I drink in the ones who have found a lively and vital spirit in our modern urbanized times. Every town holds things to love, things to dislike, and at least one thing that makes them unique. If you look closely enough, you may find treasure in those communities where it seems like the best years have passed them by.

Unlike me, Jim has no hometown. He spent his youngest years and early adulthood in coastal Georgia, but with no extended family there, he doesn't have reasons to return. His older childhood and teen years were spent in an Atlanta suburb. Subdivisions and strip malls don't make for a hometown unless you really work hard at it. Perhaps because he doesn't have my small town experience, he sometimes wishes aloud that he had a hometown. But even when you have one, like I do, the reality is the old cliche — you can't ever really go home again.

I visit my hometown often, but rarely see or do much beyond my parents' home. Most of my childhood friends moved away after high school like I did. There's no church of my chosen tradition there, no natural foods store or international grocery, and none of the many city conveniences we take for granted. Good friends and others who share my values are in ample supply up here in my neighborhood of Metro Atlanta, though. We love our church and our part of town, although the traffic gets us down sometimes. Now home is where our heart is, our ethics, our values. Hardly anyone grew up here, so we are all newcomers. It's not our hometown, but the city has become our home.

If I did ever move back to Moultrie, I doubt it would feel like home.

We love small towns on our road trips, though. It's easier to overlook their flaws when you don't know the people who live there. A quick visit gives you all the charm and none of the complexity.

A Green River and a Charming Chatauqua

As you may realize from my story about Rawlins, I'm not the biggest fan of Wyoming. Eastern Wyoming features some lovely spots, and Yellowstone is wonderful, of course. But most of Wyoming is dusty, empty, and for us, limited to interstates where people travel upwards of 85 miles per hour on a slow stretch. Not much fun.

However, one spot in mid-Wyoming charmed us. The town of Green River takes its name from the waterway running alongside the town. This source of water gave the town a greener appearance with more trees and plants than its dusty surroundings. The city had constructed some parks along the river where you could take in the view across the water to the steep cliffs beyond, if the high winds didn't blow you away. Green River was for sure one of those towns where bars outnumbered churches and seemed pretty empty, which made me wonder -- on a busy night, how many people visited each bar on average. Did locals have a preferred bar by demographic group or music preference? Or did people visit one after another and really live it up?

The funniest thing about Green River was the lunch we picked up at the local Chinese restaurant. The dish they called pepper steak was basically a pot roast dinner. Not what we were expecting, but hearty, and possibly the preference of folks who had the fortitude to make a life out here in the middle of this harsh environment.

Another charming surprise was Bay View, Michigan, where we were able to visit our friends Sue, Jim, Molly, and Patrick at their summer home. Bay View is a town that is primarily occupied only in summer, something we aren't accustomed to seeing in our neck of the woods. The town is seasonal because it is a Chautauqua.

Bay View, Michigan

Chautauqua were a form of camp meeting formed in the 19th century which were devoted as much to intellectual culture as religion or revivalism. The one in Bay View was founded in 1875 by United Methodists out of Petoskey and Grand Rapids, Michigan. Cottages were built to house the seasonal visitors, including those from other denominations, leading to an intentional, ecumenical community centered around arts, education, recreation, and religion. While traveling Chautauqua and one or two settled ones did occur in the southeast US, they are most common in the Eastern Seaboard and Great Lakes Regions. I've always been fascinated by the idea and it was wonderful to see one in person.

The adorable Victorian cottages here are not built or serviced with full utilities. To equip them for year-round living in such a cold climate so close to the winds off Lake Michigan would require serious upgrades. So every year, the town empties out around Labor Day, sitting dormant for months, only to come to life again in June. Being there just weeks after it opened for the season, we felt astoundingly fortunate to get a guided tour of the community from our friends and learn a bit about life in a Chautauqua.

The unique and seasonal nature of Bay View makes it more intriguing than most, but the town's best features can be seen in many other hamlets. Vital arts communities, opportunities for learning and recreation, active faith life — many small towns can brag of at least some of those. Turns out that our favorite places are those that have a lot in common with the Chautauqua — those towns dedicated to community learning and enrichment, close to recreation and natural beauty, and strong in community spirit. Such nice places to visit, you might want to live there!

Lake Michigan, Bay View, Michigan

It's Complicated

Small towns aren't all charms, however. Sometimes you don't even have to live in a place to discover its less savory elements.

Among endless plains of grass in central South Dakota on a back road route to the Badlands, we were suddenly amid a herd of Buffalo. The giants were snacking on the prairie all around us.

Seeking refreshment ourselves, we stopped for a break in the next town we saw on the map. Scenic, South Dakota, which is on the edge of reservation land and the Badlands, did not really live up to its name. It did, however, offer the powerful experience of seeing an old saloon that included a sign that said, *No Indians allowed, Sioux or Lakota*. A more recent owner of the bar had thankfully attempted to erase the "no" on the sign.

Old Saloon, Scenic, South Dakota

In the grocery store there, a young Native American kid worked the cash register. The shelves were bare, and we struggled to find sufficient snacks for the next leg of our journey. It may not have been scenic, but it was memorable.

On another day, we inched along behind a tractor in the middle of Nebraska. We had taken a back road to take a break from the monotony of I-80. I also wanted to stop at a dollar store to pick up a few things and figured the small towns were more likely to have one than the interstate exits. We took a turn around the downtown square in Lexington, NE after visiting their Family Dollar and found, among the usual little shops and restaurants with dated facades, a surprising sign reading — Islamic Center of Lexington.

This piqued my curiosity, finding a mosque in such a small town, and Jim was driving, so I pulled out my phone to Google. Turns out, this was a place marked by controversy over just that mosque. Lexington has a sizable Somali immigrant population these days, thanks to local meatpacking plants that employ many recent immigrants and refugees.

A group of these workers wanted a place to practice their faith and so bought a space that had recently been a laundromat. When they began holding prayers five times a day, the town told them to stop due to parking and zoning issues.

The day we visited, there were more empty spaces than full along the streets and in the public lots. Whole streets had no one parked on them. There also appeared to be plenty of churches scattered around. In this town they may have even outnumbered the bars.

So it's easy to understand why the mosque leaders and members perceived these protests as Islamophobic. The ACLU got involved, citing federal law that zoning ordinances can't restrict freedom of religion. Long-time residents, mostly white, talked about the Somalis negatively, calling them rude and insular. The lawyer representing the mosque received hate mail. Eventually the mosque was allowed, but the conflict left behind hard feelings on both sides.

And there are now two mosques in downtown Lexington. On our way out of Lexington, we saw a random plastic horse on the roof of a downtown shop. Quirky, charming, and yes, complicated.

Where I grew up, in a small town in Southwest Georgia, community spirit and boosterism lived alongside racism and insularity. As a kid, I couldn't help but question why we had segregated elementary schools long after Brown vs. Board of Education, and why our neighborhoods and churches were also segregated. Asking those questions out loud to anyone but my parents was poorly received.

At the same time, the community enthusiastically supported the singular and fully integrated high school in all its competitions and activities. The one small private school in town went out of business when I was little, so we were all in it together by the time we got to high school. There was also a vibrant arts center only a few blocks away from a public rec center with tennis courts and a pool. I was able to take art, music, dance, and be in plays. I took tennis and was a cheerleader for peewee football teams, with kids of every race and class.

Racist structures and attitude can persist, though, even in places with civic investment and imagination. This is one of the main challenges for small communities. Everyone knows each other, and has all their lives. Old habits and attitudes die hard, and it's easy to miss problems that are right in front of your face.

Superlative Small Towns

So what is it that makes a great small town? For us as tourists, the perfect small town is one with something of interest, a cute downtown, a few restaurants and shops, and a feeling of liveliness. People are out and about enjoying their town's amenities and taking care of business. The streets are clean, neat, and visiting doesn't require navigating a sea of strip mall parking lots but rather a more welcoming storefront and sidewalk orientation. But of course, that's only our preference as outsiders. It's hard to say what makes it great for those who live there. All the above, plus ample well-paying jobs and shopping that provides what you need without driving to a nearby city is a start. Beyond material needs, a small town with arts, culture, a diversity of entertainments, and ample options for spiritual life — a town with the spirit of Chatauqua — helps residents find fulfillment close to home. These are all just a starting place for what makes a healthy and happy community. They also provide some buffers against descending toward ghost town status over time.

What connects all these ideas is the concept of "sustainability." A sustainable community is first off healthy and resilient, across economics, the environment, and the social lives of its people. The level of sustainability is often deeply entwined with how the area was developed and continued to develop over time. According to John Ikerd, traditional development, especially in rural areas, was rooted in colonialism and exploitation. Creating wealth was the primary concern, extracting natural wealth from creation and compounding existing wealth in the hands of very few. The clearing of old growth timber for logging, tearing down a historic community school to build a new one out by the highway, the ongoing consolidation of farmland into the ownership of a few wealthy farmers, or the building of an overpass that cuts off one community from easy walkable access to a downtown business district — all of this is exploitative, not sustainable. Natural resources are exhausted, local agriculture doesn't feed the local community, and those without social capital are made ever more vulnerable. Sustainable development, on the other hand, can enable communities to grow in ways that are less exploitative, use fewer resources, and are inclusive of the broader community.

One easy example is where to build a new shopping center. Developers must choose between available land options when building a new Publix, Walmart, or mall. Most Americans have observed the phenomenon of a new shopping area developed just a short distance from where an older one sits largely empty in decline. These obsolete shopping areas are called greyfields. This contrasts with greenfields, natural areas that have not seen development. Developers prefer greenfields because cutting down trees for new construction is more affordable than renovating existing properties. When a town allows developers to clear cut greenfields rather than rehabbing greyfields, they increase blight and reduce the environmental and economic sustainability of their communities.

Theater, Windom, Minnesota

We saw our fair share of abandoned big box shopping centers and strip malls along our journey. Suffice it to say that they did not make their communities appealing to us as travelers.

Going beyond land use and conservation, sustainable communities have as their mission that all people and future generations can thrive, enjoy good health, and create a high quality of life. It takes community will for a town's leadership to make different choices. Many communities would say they currently work toward this goal, but ignore that their zoning laws favor wealth and exploitation, or allow only a few to receive these benefits.

What is this like in practice? Kaid Benfield of the NRDC describes an imagined Sustainaville with public green spaces and community gardens, diverse housing types and price points all mixed together, neighborhood shops, public transit, and walkability. It sounds like a very upscale utopia, inaccessible in most places in the US today. And of course this vision is shaped by American values around development and land use, although it goes pretty far to disturb US business-as-usual in city planning. You can imagine how this can become a consumer product, with sustainable livable communities accessible to those with wealth while all others live much differently.

Mural, Ashland, Wisconsin

Yet small towns have an advantage here. In a small town, everyone is in the same water, even if they're not in the same boat. One county commission or town council, one school system, one downtown. Everyone is in it together, and everyone benefits if the community makes sustainable choices so that all can access the benefits of sustainability. In the end, it all comes back to community. The key to efforts like this is civic life. In other words, a group of people who care enough to try something new.

In Robert Putnam's book, *Bowling Alone*, the author's research shows the decline of almost every form of community organization in the United States, and that people are joining organizations less and retreating into private worlds of their own making. Robert Bellah and his coauthors, in *Habits of the Heart: Individualism and Commitment in American Life*, took this further and identified the negative impacts of individualism on our lives in community. When freedom is identified as breaking free from communities and structures, all meaning and convictions that are derived from the gifts of community are lost.

In my work and faith as a progressive Christian, I can't help but envision the potential for building sustainable communities in the values of progressive faith. As we try to orient ourselves toward hope, and put that hope in action to build sustainability, we can gather in what Ross Smillie calls, "anticipatory communities." These can be faith communities, but don't have to be. They can also be groups of concerned local citizens who are connected by their longings for things to get better.

Anticipatory communities are those that provide an example of the different world we long to see. In history, these have ranged from isolated communities of monks dedicating their life to prayer, to 19th century American utopias, to modern communes. In one of my favorite South Georgia examples, Koinonia Farm sought to be a demonstration plot for the kingdom of God. Initially, this meant racial integration, and over time, it evolved into environmentally sound farming and intentional living. Living toward the future we want to see is one way to make it a reality.

As much as I love all small towns, the ones that are more sustainable are more enjoyable to us as travelers. The best towns have lovely parks and walking paths, interesting architecture that is well-maintained, and vital local economies. In those towns, we can enjoy a sidewalk cafe downtown without feeling like the only remaining people on earth. We can take a walk after that meal and see beautiful things. We don't have to spend money on an attraction or tourist trap to have a good time. We can be happy tourists because of the very same things that make a town good for its residents.

In some ways, I think it would be better if we could all be tourists a bit in the places that we live. Get out of our normal routines. Enjoy more of the good things and brag about them to others on social media or face to face. Eat at that sidewalk cafe, go to the local museum, walk the trail along the old railroad tracks. See it all with fresh eyes. And if you don't see any good things, be a part of creating them. Become anticipatory in your own corner of the world.

We tourists also need to be more like residents. Drive past the chains and patronize local businesses. Pick up trash you see around the streets. Say hello and get to know those you pass on the walking trail. Let local leaders know what you loved about their town and why.

Years ago, at a Georgia Interfaith Power and Light banquet, when our church at the time was receiving an award for our work to make our building and systems more environmentally responsible. The rabbi of the congregation hosting us told us this story:

> "The righteous man, Honi, once encountered a man planting a carob tree. 'How long will it take to bear fruit?' he inquired. 'About 70 years,' the man replied. 'So, you think you will live long enough to taste its fruits?' The man explained, 'I have found ready-grown carob trees in the world. As my forefathers planted them for me, so I plant for my children.'"

When we travel, how do we plant trees for the future? If we all work together, tourists, residents, every one of us, maybe we can make every place we encounter a little more sustainable.

| 9 |

Lesson Nine: Home by Another Road

Our van shuddered as the dirt road's ridges deepened the further we went into the woods. Trusting only the sign we passed a half-hour ago, since our signal had been lost 50 miles inland from here, we quickly bounced from wanting to turn back to wanting to persist. Our discussions became only about this decision. There was no more small talk on the way to this roadside attraction. The thing that kept us going, really, was the fact that the road had narrowed and the ditches deepened such that turning would have been difficult at best. The miles of trees were suddenly interrupted by the disorienting sight of a bright orange tent not too far into the woods. We had read that camping was allowed out here, but after millions of pine trees in the neat rows of a timber farm, anything other than a pine tree was startling. We kept driving. Our reward, such that it was, turned out to be only the picture we took at the sign which led us down this strange and desolate track. The wooden and weathered sign read — The Beginning of US Highway 41.

Beginning of US 41 Sign, Copper Harbor, Michigan

For us, though, and particularly for me, after younger years rambling about the back roads of south Georgia and Florida, this felt more like an end than a beginning.

Growing up a short drive away from the legendary Highway 41, my love affair with old roads began early. I was drawn to those old low slung motels I would see out the car window when we took the back ways, the old ways, that led to Florida sunshine or westward ho. Later, as a young driver, my curious mind couldn't help notice signs for Thigpen Trail, Old Mail Road or Federal Road, now just two-lane faded pavement or dirt tracks through empty countryside. The idea of people traveling these paths for hundreds of years before me took me on numerous fanciful trips in covered wagons or on stagecoaches dusty with the clay-sand dirt that predated them by millennia.

Many of these roads were merely covering older Native American trails of trade and travel. Kennard's Trail through southern Worth County was part of a network of trails connecting Creek villages from the Chattahoochee to the east coast of Georgia. The old Coffee Road through what the settlers called frontier in south central Georgia was then cut and built by slaves and carried weapons used to drive the Creek Indians off their land. From this unjust history to the Allman Brothers' ode to a man who can't stay put or stay faithful, Highway 41 is certainly a mixed bag.

Of course, Highway 41, while looming large in the memory of this south Georgia girl, and well-known thanks to the Allman Brothers song, pales in reputation alongside the O.G. American highway, Route 66.

When we realized on our way south one year that one of our homeward routes could align us, if briefly, with Route 66, this highway-loving girl's heart skipped a beat. Visions of old roadside motels, kitschy gas stations, and diners as far as the eye could see filled my brain. I booked us into a Route 66 themed vacation rental (motels were challenging with the dogs) and wove this junket into our itinerary.

As with all things, the reality was both worse than, and better than, the fantasy. Firstly, finding old Route 66 is a challenge. Since it is now overshadowed or literally paved over by newer four lanes and interstates, we and our map apps were challenged with constant twisty turns simply to stay on or reconnect to short segments of the historic highway. When we did find it, it was as underwhelming as some parts of Highway 41 would be to the uninitiated. Long stretches of strip malls or fields gave way to yet another choice point where we would inevitably fall off the old road and have to find our way back.

There were bright spots along the way. An old gas station, building restored and red vintage pumps gleaming, sat as a museum to the early days of auto travel. I could easily picture a fella hanging out in a tight white tee shirt and jeans, bandanna in his pocket, cigarettes rolled up in his sleeve, waiting around for someone to pull up for his gas pumping services. Or maybe I've just seen too many old movies.

Ambler's Texaco Gas Station, Dwight, Illinois

The grave of Mother Jones, freshly laid with flowers and tributes from those seeking to remember this labor leader, made us think about the intersection of historical labor organizing with roads and the cars that traversed them. The Ariston Cafe, a little diner in Litchfield, IL open since the 1930s in its current location, and longer than that if you count a few moves before, allowed us to sit where countless have sat over the years, grabbing supper and friendly conversation along their long journeys. A little museum down the road explained in exhibits and photos how the road shaped the community of Litchfield, and how that connection came at a cost as Route 66 travel shifted to the interstates that passed it by.

Other attractions on our brief Route 66 journey were tacky and underwhelming.

Antique Mall, Route 66, Illinois

After being spoiled by all the big gas plazas along interstates, on these back roads it was hard to find a gas station with a clean restroom. The route was challenging to follow at the best of times, making us question every turn. We gave up and got back on the interstate after our millionth encounter with a dead end.

The new road won the day.

Roads change. And roads can change you.

#VanChurch

For a book called #vanchurch, I haven't talked much about church. In fact, we rarely attend traditional church services on our travels. We pray in chapels, walk labyrinths, and worship in the cathedral of the woods, but there are very few hymns and sermons along the way.

Yet we still found faith on the road. Not only in the practices above, but also in the simple experience of place. The idea that places change you is biblical, after all. There's no Moses leading the Israelites out of slavery without first standing barefoot on the dirt that became holy ground when the bush burned. There's no Letter to the Corinthians without Paul losing his sight in the light on the road to Damascus. There's not a single Beatitude without Jesus first standing on the mount to speak to the crowd. And in my favorite Bible verse, the Magi only make it out alive after visiting Jesus by going "home by another road."

This speaks to the spiritually transformative power of travel. By that I mean, travel can change your spirit. But it takes work to cultivate this change, and it takes paying attention to help change find root in our souls.

On only the second day of our #vanlife, we were avoiding a torrential thunderstorm by taking the slow route along a back road. As the rain began to slack off, we encountered a much slower and older form of transport. I've always been interested in the Amish, but I never expected to find Amish teenagers cruising a gas station on a back road in Kentucky. Their vehicles of choice were not cars, but horse-drawn buggies. The gas station was long closed, which made no difference to their horsepower. These teens, with buggies pulled side by side and deep in conversation, reminded me to keep my eyes open for children of God even in the most unexpected of places.

Churches, Museums, and Shrines

While I discovered spirit all along our journey, we did encounter a few more traditional church spaces and institutions. One of the first intersections of our trip with religious traditions was Elvis Presley's family church, which had been moved to the site of his childhood home in Tupelo, MS. The 1930s-era Assembly of God congregation held Pentecostal worship, involving lively music and much singing and shouting, which was all highly influential on the later musical stylings of the flamboyant Elvis. We heard the sounds of this experience at this tiny white frame church building — they play a recording of it every half hour.

In Eureka Springs, AR, we found evidence of another modern religious culture at the Passion Play and Creation Museum. The Passion Play is an outdoor reenactment of the final days of Jesus' life, as depicted in the Bible. Editorialized for drama, of course, and over the centuries there has been a sad history of Passion Plays being used to foment hatred of Jews and other minority groups. So not just good fun.

In addition to the giant amphitheater where the play is held, the site contains a reconstruction of the Holy Land that you can walk through and meet characters from the Bible, several museums and galleries, a campground, a piece of the Berlin wall, a bomb shelter from Israel, and last but not least, a giant Jesus known as Christ of the Ozarks. As fascinating as this 67 foot figure with outstretched arms was to me, it felt much more neutral and agenda-free than the rest of the attractions, museums and galleries.

Christ of the Ozarks, Eureka Springs, Arkansas

One museum in particular gave me much to ponder. According to their own website:

> "This Cultural and Biblical History Museum provides a brief snapshot of the history of creation and mankind and how the Bible fits into that as well as providing evidences (apologetics) for God's existence as well as why Christian theism and the Bible provide the most logical and plausible worldview of existence. *Many free items are available to help 'the believer think and the thinker to believe.'"

This history museum had a definite agenda. Things from scientific and historical record were presented as possibilities alongside Biblical creationism, with a "You decide!" attitude. Were there dinosaurs? You decide! Did they live at the same time as people? You decide! Is the earth millions of years old or only a few thousand? You decide! And so on.

As I imagine I am the "thinker" in their mission statement, but also a believing progressive Christian, the only thing this museum convinced me to believe is that there is a bubble within which many live, never exposed to how science actually works. While I could certainly paint these museum organizers with the brush of being uninformed or resistant to scientific consensus, I can also say that many of my liberal friends and neighbors in metro Atlanta have never been to a museum like this. Visiting the museum was a border crossing for me, to be sure. I had to set my judgmental hat aside and accept that this was something that many found meaningful, and think about their point of view for at least a little while.

In fact, the other museums on the grounds highlighted how much I have in common with those for whom this place is sacred and meaningful. The Sacred Arts center holds religious art from around the world and from many eras throughout history. The icons and paintings filled me with emotion and inspiration, as do those I see in the High Museum in Atlanta. The Bible Museum holds rare Bible texts and translations. While I was concerned with the storage and conditions, knowing how fragile rare texts can be, I loved looking at the historic Bibles, as much as I love seeing similar collections in the library at Candler Theology School at Emory, where I went to seminary. The

Bible and its history, and the ways people show their devotion through creativity, are incredibly important to me — to my faith, my career, and my life. Every other person wandering these exhibits likely felt the same, even as their Christian faith may provide very different beliefs and values than mine.

On the other side of Eureka Springs, we visited the architecturally stunning Thorncrown Chapel, built by Jim Reed and designed by E. Fay Jones to take full advantage of the heavenly mountain views its site provides. Only 40 years old, the non-denominational chapel is dedicated to helping people "encounter not just a beautiful building, but the God who longs to fill your life with the beauty of His presence." Reed built the chapel after realizing the number of strangers who drove onto his land to take in the views. Someone else might have put up a gate to keep them out, but Reed decided to create a place for them to stop and rest. There is no fee to visit, embodying the mission of its creator to provide a place of peace for the many people who once came up the drive simply to enjoy God's cathedral of natural beauty.

After parking, we walked up a trail through the woods to get a glimpse of the chapel itself. The all glass walls bring the surrounding oaks and pines inside this sanctuary. The soaring rafters overhead point the way right up to heaven. There were few others in and around the chapel, so I took the opportunity to sit and meditate while Jim walked the dogs. While natural beauty is always enough for me to have a spiritual experience, architecture like Thorncrown supplies another kind of awe. The creativity and artistry of architects and builders is a true gift from God, and one that provided a bit of church for me at Thorncrown.

In Baraga, MI, there is a shrine to the man known as the Snowshoe Priest, or Bishop Frederic Baraga, who came from Slovenia in 1830 to serve the Catholic missions in the area. Modern in architecture, like Thorncrown, the slightly run-down shrine also soars into the trees. Spider-like arches with tepee shaped foundations hold in their center a statue of Baraga, supporting a 60-foot copper statue of the priest standing on a cloud, holding his snowshoes and a cross. Baraga's legacy is complicated by the long-ranging effects of Europeans like Baraga on the Native Americans in these lands. Our fellow worshipers at this religious site were primarily mosquitos, who didn't exactly encourage us to linger. This shrine overlooking Lake Superior was unique, if nothing else.

By the time we made it to Salt Lake City after seven long days of driving and camping, church was the last thing on our mind. We were road-weary and I had altitude sickness from our time in the Wasatch range. After settling in to our motel (always an adventure navigating interior hallways with a dog or two in tow) the last thing I wanted to do was get back out in traffic. After a few days of rest, though, on Sunday morning I leashed Poppy and stepped out into the city, ready to explore whatever it had to offer.

Pride Parade, Salt Lake City, Utah

Turns out, I was walking along the route of the Salt Lake City Pride parade. It went on and on, rivaling Atlanta's in length, if not in crowd numbers. Poppy and I settled in on a grassy hill near the Convention Center as the floats and groups rolled and walked by. The official Church of Latter Day Saints did not have a float, and the conservative positions of that church on gay marriage are very public. But I saw a contingent carrying signs marked Mormons Building Bridges, followed by Episcopalian, Buddhist, Jewish, Baptist, and Lutheran congregations, all proclaiming God's love for everyone.

I may not have been in a church building, but that Sunday morning felt a lot like church.

Sunday School on the Road

We can't have church without spiritual formation. While there were no classes at 9:30 on Sunday mornings during our trip, we were constantly learning. The main curriculum at the Sunday School of #vanchurch is how to love our neighbors by loving our neighbors' land as much as we love my own.

Travel has broadened my sense of what is "my land." The little corner of Georgia where I grew up or my neighborhood in metro Atlanta are only a small piece of the land to which I feel connected. My love and connection now range from the Rocky Mountains to the Great Lakes to the length of the Missouri River. Even if I didn't feel such affection for the many lands that make up the US, I know that loving all land as if it were my own yard will build a better future. Avoiding damage, keeping it free from trash, protecting it from occupation or exploitation--all this becomes transferable to every piece of land within our borders and beyond.

It shouldn't take a cross-country road trip to realize this, but now that my eyes are opened, my heart is sealed with this sense of love and mutuality. In the end, if I truly love my neighbor, I must love their land. Not in a simple way, but complex, intersectional, interfaith, justice-minded, and global.

In this conviction I felt a new land ethic emerging. In my environmental philosophy courses back in college, we talked about developing our own land ethics or frameworks for how we relate to our environment as individuals, communities, and as a nation.

Practicing #VanChurch

Ethics and spirituality only go so far, though, if they aren't put into practice. To be transformed, research suggests we must first be disoriented, then reflective, and then practice in ways that incorporate new insights into our daily lives. The practice of traveling in search of spiritual and ethical insights is to layer spiritual attention on all those experiences that have the potential to awaken us to new realities. One way to do that is through spiritual practices that go back to the earliest days of the Judeo-Christian faith.

We can be prayerful and mindful. We can take the time to observe in each place who and what we are really seeing. One of Jesus' gifts to us is how he saw the people behind their personal challenges. Whether oppressed, outcast, or having a disability, he saw them all as beloved children of God. We too can look at those along our journey with eyes of love, and say a quick prayer for all we encounter.

We can take up ancient prayer practice of lament. If we encounter a place that seems bleak and damaged, we can name the things we are grieving about our communities, the land we inhabit, and the earth as a whole.

We can also lean into confession. Confession gets a bad rap. It is assumed to be a way to beat yourself up for mistakes and flaws. Few of us need much help with that. But confession (or praying to acknowledge ways we have fallen short) can actually be a profound experience of naming truths and history so we can go forward by another road.

We can practice Sabbath. Sabbath, in ancient Israel, was both the practice of resting one day a week and practices like letting land rest, forgiving debts, and acting in sustainable ways with others in the community. When we take time to rest and restore ourselves and others, our communities are strengthened.

We can lean into hope. It can be hard to hope when our communities and countries seem to be in decline. But hope may be the only thing that will save us. Resignation leads to passivity, while hope leads to changed actions. In this way communal hope, the hope of many, can change whole communities.

Whether you are road tripping or simply traveling this journey called life, I believe that with a little work, anyone can find transformation along the way. It only takes a willingness to get out of your comfort zone, the will to incorporate a bit of spiritual practice every day, and an openness to the new things you are learning.

#VanChurch helped teach me these lessons. I now use them every day, including days when I don't travel farther than my mailbox. You, too, can find yourselves traveling a new road, changed by the journey.

| 10 |

Lost and Found: A Postscript

Lost:
A dog bed
Two phone chargers
Three pieces of shelf hardware
Five nights of sleep
Numerous phone chargers
That new van smell
A tight grip on our schedules
The illusion of control
Fear of the unfamiliar

Found:
A new dog bed
Two car seat heating pads
Three bottles of sunscreen
Eight stickers for the back of the van
Nine souvenirs for loved ones
Too many ticks
Magnets from every state we visited
Infinite pamphlets and maps
A willingness to take risks
A feeling that we could handle anything
Courage to take the road less traveled

It is impossible to say what our lives would be like today if we hadn't gotten lost and found ourselves again through our travels.

There was no way of imagining the road ahead when we started our #vanlife journeys in May 2018. Even early in 2020 when we began planning our third van trip (which still hasn't happened), we never imagined that we would soon face a global pandemic. In addition to this worldwide collective chaos, over the last few years our little family has also navigated the challenging roads of dealing with dog broken bones, a human concussion, a case of shingles, mental health challenges, and all the usual trials of day-to-day life and work. I can't say for sure what those challenges would have felt like without so many miles in our rear-view mirror, but I believe the lessons from our journeys helped us every day.

Whenever we didn't know what to do next, we:

- Spent time in nature
- Looked to history for lessons on resilience
- Took time to center even when life took a detour
- Faced the present with realism while drawing maps to our desired futures
- Remembered that we could face anything, together.

Because of those lessons from our journeys, in 2021 we made another major job and lifestyle change when Jim retired early to help me publish books. A bonus was that we could spend more time on the road once it was safer to travel. I wonder if we would have taken the new road of launching our publishing company without first taking the risk of exploring new roads across the US. I wonder if I would have had the nerve to put out these first few books if I had not strengthened that nerve through storms, bugs, and temper tantrums along the way. Travel gave us gifts that somehow, some way, got us through the past few years without losing our resolve and our faith.

To sum up, we persisted.

That persistence of putting one foot in front of the other was learned by the constant moving forward of our life on the road. We are already planning our next trips, now that we've learned to live with this new normal of late pandemic life. I can't begin to predict what lessons those travels will bring us.

But we can't wait to find out.

Elkhorn Ranch Unit, Teddy Roosevelt National Park, Medora, North Dakota

31 Days of #VanChurch Devotions

Find Your Place - Day 1

In #VanChurch, I talk a lot about how our life situation informed our travels, as well as where we were starting geographically and where we hoped to end up. As travelers on the journey of life, we are not always where we want to be at any given moment, geographically or metaphorically. Yet the first step of a successful journey is knowing where we are.

How would you use a map to draw your current situation? Draw or write about it below:

Find Your Place - Day 2

I mention in Chapter 2 that I attended a conference where the leader asked us all to identify ourselves as hailing from a land that was first inhabited by those who came before us, and a land that is fundamentally connected to the way the water flows above it. For example, I am typing these words on the lands of the Creek Indians and alongside the divide line of the Peachtree Creek to Chattahoochee River watershed. This is one way of seeing our location and understanding where we are in life.

What is your geographical place right now? Describe it below.

Find Your Place - Day 3

Another way of pinpointing where we are is tracing the history that brought us into being and sustained us to this day. Telling our family stories, our origin stories, our stories of how we came to be in this specific place on this specific day can give us so much insight into who we are and where we start our journey.

What stories inform your current situation and/or location?

Find Your Place - Day 4

A fourth way of identifying our current location is reading texts that have been seen as sacred, wisdom-bearing, or life-giving for our communities. For me, these come from the Bible, from favorite books, movies, tv shows, and from other sacred texts.

What stories have meaning for you? Write about them below:

Find Your Place - Day 5

We may not like where we are very much at all. But to move forward, we have to start here and now, accepting the reality of our current location and situation. To accept where we are, we may have to let go of our ideas about where we should be. Radical acceptance is an approach rooted in Buddhism and psychology that promotes acceptance as helpful for spiritual and psychological wellness. Radical acceptance fits well into my Christian faith, as I believe that God loves us just as we are right now. Even when the world is not as it should be, we are all loved and accepted as we are. Our challenge is to believe in that love and accept ourselves as God accepts us.

What are you struggling to accept about your life right now?

Find Your Place - Day 6

When we think of the foundational stories of the Christian faith, those involving the disciples after Jesus' death can serve as examples of radical acceptance. They could not believe the things that were occurring, yet stepped out on faith to meet the risen Jesus as they encountered him, at meals, on a boat, in the upper room. They were initially terrified by these strange events but found a way to be present to them.

What is hardest to face about the reality of your situation right now? How can you be more present to it even as it disturbs you?

Make a Map - Day 7

Now that you have a bit of an idea of where you are, the next step is determining where you need or want to go. I wanted to go West. We needed to be out west for work for one week, and so that helped us define the start and end points of our journey. I was able to mark those on a map. Google Maps, to be exact. Out of all the possible routes and stops between Atlanta and Salt Lake City, I marked the ones I would most like to see. Unfortunately, we don't have Google Maps for our own futures. So before we can determine where on the map we want to go, we must draw the rest of the map ourselves. We have to figure out all the possible routes and stops for our journey together.

What is the first thing that comes to mind when you think of your future? Where would you like to be in 2 years? How would you like to be feeling? What would you like to be doing?

Make a Map - Day 8

Another good place to start is with stories of movement and change. On our trip, we learned of the movements of indigenous Americans, explorers, immigrants, and others. We also saw the movements and changes of nature across seasons and ecosystems. You may have stories from your family, stories portrayed by your favorite books, movies, and TV shows, and stories of those who inspire and challenge you today and throughout history. But these are only a few possibilities, and the right stories for you will emerge as you travel.

What stories of movement and change inspire you?

Make a Map - Day 9

Once you draw a map of possible routes, how will you know which roads to travel? Well, those will come from your values and goals. Knowing who you are and who you want to be will make your traveling decisions easier and your path ahead clearer.

What are your most strongly held values and beliefs? What are you most passionate about?

Cross Your Rubicon - Day 10

For our trips, I also had to figure out how long we could be gone, how much money we could spare, and what resources we had available for our journey. In your life journey, the possibilities are as wide as your imagination. Yet we all have some bounds on any journey.

- How much energy or fuel can we spend?
- What resources can we use for the road ahead?
- How much time do we have or are willing to give to the journey?

To measure the resources you can use for your journey, inventories can be helpful.

What are your greatest gifts? What are you good at? What gifts live among your friends and family that can be helpful for your journey?

Cross Your Rubicon - Day 11

How can you fuel your journey with mental and physical attention and energy? Too often our busy lives prevent us from having what we need to take forward steps. The only remedy for this is to cut back your life to the essentials, firstly those things that are necessary for health, safety and basic needs, with the addition of a few activities that align with your personal mission and values. It is a challenge to streamline but will pay dividends beyond imagining. Take the time, if you need it, to listen and wait. Get a little less busy, if necessary. Sometimes the most interesting things happen in the pauses.

What do you need to put aside so that you have time and energy for your journey? Consider all non-essentials and make a list below.

Cross Your Rubicon - Day 12

Another source of fuel is community. Gather with others. Share stories, discuss your journeys, be vulnerable about fears and concerns. Fellow travelers, even if on roads not quite like our own, can be an invaluable source of support. How can you fuel your journey with community?

What person or group can you ask to support you on your journey? How will you ask them to help?

Be a Stranger in a Strange Land - Day 13

Life doesn't always turn out like we planned. And – it is okay to be exactly who we are—broken and beautiful and complex! Until we take an honest look at where we are and who we are, it will be almost impossible to take our next steps toward where we want to be.

What are the biggest challenges facing you right now?

Be a Stranger in a Strange Land - Day 14

It is so challenging to find transformation in our life or travel journeys when we are already feeling off-center, buffeted by the winds of life. Some key shifts in time and energy can make a huge impact on our ability to learn along the way.

When you think of change, does it make you feel energized or tired? If tired, why? Write about those feelings below.

Find Your Center - Day 15

We are often spread too thin to lean into the new things we encounter along our journeys. Think of the way your job can feel when doing the work of two people due to vacancy or cutbacks. The mere idea of a new software system or form to complete to do your work feels overwhelming. We can be the same when facing new experiences from a place of exhaustion. But once you are less exhausted, you will be better able to sit with disorientation and embrace new insights as they come along.

Are you exhausted? Why? What can you do today to find some rest and restoration?

Find Your Center - Day 16

We are not alone on our journeys, but too often we act as if we are. Exhaustion and constant activity prevent connection with those who could be our travel companions. Find your people, and make time for them. One more task checked off the list is less important than building a fabric of support for any change you are facing now or will face in the future.

What one person could you call for support on your journey right now? Who else? Make a list of them and any others you can rely on. How can you make that list longer? What is getting in the way of connecting with others in your life right now?

Brake for Delight - Day 17

It is easy to miss the delightful in our lives. To see what we are missing, we have to make space in our daily activities for pauses, meditation, prayer. Open eyes often come from a place of centeredness within us, one that is difficult to find if we are constantly in motion. This was particularly true on our trips, with the whirlwind of getting from place to place and setting up camp every night. Our commitment to finding labyrinths, botanical gardens, and other places that grounded and centered us made all the difference.

What delightful things have you seen this week? How can you make space in your life to notice more?

Brake for Delight - Day 18

Spiritual experiences are all along our journeys, if we are able to see them. Like delight, they can be easy to miss if we are too busy or exhausted. A great way to see more of the spiritual is to journal every day, like you are doing in this devotional guide. Write your answers to the following questions today, and then make a practice of doing that every evening before bed, or every day at lunch. You may be surprised at what you see.

Where did you feel or experience something spiritual today or this week? What was that like? Describe it in detail here.

Brake for Delight - Day 19

Delight and spirit are amplified when we talk to others about ways they are experiencing their journeys. Regular reflection with literal or metaphorical travel companions helps us keep our eyes open. Their stories also show us things we might not see ourselves.

Who in your life is a good partner for sharing stories of spirit and delight? How will you start doing so regularly?

Lose Your Place - Day 20

Detours are ever present on road trips like ours. Seeking the less-beaten paths of back roads and byways means finding some of them in no condition for travel. It is hard to become accustomed to the inevitability of detours. We are trained in our modern lives to seek the fastest route our GPS or app can identify and avoid delays and detours wherever possible. Taking a more scenic (aka slower) path goes against all the algorithms and requires telling your GPS to shut up multiple times per day.

How do you typically feel when your planned direction is detoured? In travel? In life?

Lose Your Place - Day 21

One of my favorite prayer mantras is "Be still and know that I am God." It serves as a powerful touchstone to remind me to find stillness and accept the reality I am facing before taking further action. Tara Brach, in her book Radical Acceptance (2003), suggests that quiet periods of guided reflection and meditation can help with resting in such stillness. These times of quiet can also help make room in our brains for coping with detours, spotting delight and spirit along our ways.

Do you meditate? If not, why not start today? Use the mantra above to focus on while breathing mindfully. Do it for a minute or five or even fifteen. Write down how it felt to meditate below:

Lose Your Place - Day 22

Detours can be both frustrating and beautiful, a gift in the unexpected things they bring to our attention. We backtracked and went around an area where a lake had covered the road only to find an adorable town which was giving away free land to anyone who would settle and work in the town (read: pay taxes) for a number of years. We had to do a U-turn on a dirt road that turned into a field, but we learned our van can navigate almost any road successfully, and that knowledge helped us believe that we have the skills to manage whatever we face on our journey.

Was there a time in your life when a detour brought unexpected gifts? What did the detour feel like initially? What gifts did it eventually bring? When and how did you become aware of those gifts?

Lose Your Place - Day 23

The detours of travel, and the detours of life, are prime time for learning and growth. During times of change, we are called to leave old roads behind. In fact, the story of Jesus is the story of a community who thought things would go one way, toward a future as a community following a beloved rabbi around, hearing his teachings and loving their neighbors under his guidance—only to find their leader killed by political forces. They were forced to make a new way without him.

Have you ever had to pivot and find a new way when faced with an unexpected detour on the road or in life? What skills or resources did you use to find that new way? What did you learn from that experience?

Lose Your Place - Day 24

Getting into unfamiliar territory on the road or in your life brings new experiences, impressions, and information. This is great, because getting outside our comfort zone can bring us new insights and change our ways of thinking. It is an uphill battle, though. Have you heard of confirmation bias? One of the reasons getting outside our comfort zone is so good for learning is because we are programmed to favor information that reinforces our current beliefs. In everyday life, we typically seek out facts that only confirm what we already believe. Our brains actually light up in the pleasure centers when we find new sources of information that back up our existing opinions! This is why it can be so difficult to learn new things.

Have you ever found yourself trying to fit a disorienting experience into your existing ways of thinking? Describe that experience. What did it feel like mentally? Physically? What conversations did you have with yourself?

Lose Your Place - Day 25

The trick to avoiding confirmation bias is noticing it and calling it out. The next time you are traveling or trying something new, I challenge you to pay close attention to those things that feel uncomfortable. Don't put yourself in danger or anything! But it is often in our mental discomfort that we can see our tendency toward confirmation bias. Once we encounter discomfort, we fight the bias toward quick resolution by simply sitting with the discomfort for a while.

When was the last time you encountered an idea that seemed unfamiliar and troubling? Take a minute to remember that experience in detail. What did that experience feel like? How did the new idea conflict with your current way of seeing the world? Sit with that contradiction for a few minutes, acknowledging the conflict. How did that sitting feel?

Lose Your Place - Day 26

Faced with new information and experiences, it can be all too easy to ignore new insights and stick with our preconceptions. But sometimes, just taking a moment to pause can interrupt our confirmation bias and open us to new ways of seeing. Even when our GPS app sent us down a road that was no more than two ruts in a field, pausing revealed the next right step. Otherwise, we'd still be sitting out in that field today. We stopped, gave it some thought, and figured out how to turn around without getting bogged down. Teamwork helped with the 11-point turn, but only keeping our eyes open to possibility helped us find the right spot.

In the future, how can you pause when you encounter new experiences or information to leave room for new insights?

Stay Rooted and Keep Branching - Day 27

Roots are a good thing. They ground us in a place and community and make us who we are, whether we are rooted in our family or community of birth or in a chosen family and village.

What gifts have you received from your roots?

Stay Rooted and Keep Branching - Day 28

Roots only become a challenge when they keep us in one place forever. It's normal to want to stay in familiar territory. It feels safe where we are. Moving means risking, and we don't know if we can take any more loss or pain.

When have you found yourself choosing safety over taking risks? Were those all good choices?

Stay Rooted and Keep Branching - Day 29

God loves us even when we are root-bound. We are invited to stay hidden under God's wings for as long as we need to. However, God also has big visions and dreams for us that can't be lived into if we stay stuck.

How do you listen to God's call for your life? What will you do if it calls you out of safety into uncertainty?

Stay Rooted and Keep Branching - Day 30

Listening and taking risks is practically impossible if we are hurting or depleted. Often the first thing we have to do is feed our roots and heal.

How can you find healing sustenance right now in your family, friends, and community? What will you do this week to draw on their resources and gifts so you will be ready to branch beyond?

Home by Another Road - Day 31

Even if we figure out our calling toward something new, it can be hard to figure out what to do next in that direction. It can be hard to see the signs if we are not used to looking for them. They may not be the kind of signs we expect. They may require going inward to find the next leg of our journey, or outward to brainstorm it with our beloved community of family and friends. We may have to wait, remaining open to seeing that next right turn when it appears.

What will you do this week to look for directional signs in your life? Will you go inward through meditation and prayer? Will you brainstorm with your people? Will you pause, with eyes open, to see what appears? Write your plan below.

NOTES

References and Location Information are listed in the order in which they appear in the chapter.

Lesson Three

Land Between the Lakes Natural Recreation Area, Kentucky. Retrieved August 1, 2022, from https://landbetweenthelakes.us/

"Mississippi River" *American Rivers,* www.americanrivers.org/river/mississippi-river/.

Arrow Rock (U.S. National Park Service), Missouri. *National Park Service,* www.nps.gov/places/arrow-rock.htm.

"Missouri River" *American Rivers,* www.americanrivers.org/river/missouri-river/.

"Moncacht-Apé" *Wikipedia,* 10 May 2012, en.wikipedia.org/wiki/Moncacht-Apé.

"Lewis & Clark Expedition" *National Archives,* 15 Aug. 2016, www.archives.gov/education/lessons/lewis-clark.

The Sioux City Lewis & Clark Interpretive Center, Sioux City, Iowa. https://www.siouxcitylcic.com/

Fort Mandan, Washburn, North Dakota, https://www.nps.gov/places/fort-mandan.htm

Dignity, Chamberlain, South Dakota, "The Story of Dignity: of Earth & Sky" *Travel South Dakota,* www.travelsouthdakota.com/trip-ideas/story/dignity-earth-sky.

Gonzalez, Fernando. "Elias's 'River': A Simple But Satisfying Flow" *The Washington Post*, 19 Sept. 2004, www.washingtonpost.com/archive/lifestyle/style/2004/09/19/eliass-river-a-simple-but-satisfying-flow/41a04c78-d2b3-4743-a38c-096923d1327b/.

"Watershed Map Chattahoochee Riverkeeper" chattahoochee.org/watershed-map/.

Anderson, Brett. "Gulf Oysters Are Dying, Putting a Southern Tradition at Risk" *The New York Times*, 12 Nov. 2019, www.nytimes.com/2019/11/12/dining/gulf-oysters.html.

Carter, President Jimmy. "The Allure of the Altamaha" *The Nature Conservancy*, 31 Aug. 2012, www.nature.org/en-us/magazine/magazine-articles/the-allure-of-the-altamaha/.

"Salt Marshes" *Oceans, Coasts & Seashores (U.S. National Park Service)*, www.nps.gov/subjects/oceans/salt-marshes.htm.

Lesson Four

Ingalls Homestead: Laura's Living Prairie, De Smet, South Dakota, https://www.ingallshomestead.com/

McLemore, Laura. "Historical Perspective or Racism in ?" *Little House on the Prairie*, 7 Dec. 2018, littlehouseontheprairie.com/historical-perspective-or-racism-in-little-house-on-the-prairie.

Linsenmayer, Penny T. "A Study of Laura Ingalls Wilder's Little House on the Prairie" *Kansas Historical Society*, Autumn 2001, https://www.kshs.org/publicat/history/2001autumn_linsenmayer.pdf. www.kshs.org/publicat/history/2001autumn_linsenmayer.pdf.

Akta Lakota Museum, Chamberlain, South Dakota. https://aktalakota.stjo.org/

Chapel, St. Joseph's Indian School, Chamberlain, South Dakota. https://www.stjo.org/chapel/

Oklahoma. 1943. https://rodgersandhammerstein.com/show/oklahoma/

"Milestones: 1830-1860 Indian Treaties" *Office of the Historian*, history.state.gov/milestones/1830-1860/indian-treaties.

Burrough, Bryan. "The myth of Alamo gets the history all wrong" *The Washington Post*, 10 June 2021, www.washingtonpost.com/outlook/2021/06/10/myth-alamo-gets-history-all-wrong/.

"Pre-Civil War African-American Slavery | National Expansion and Reform, 1815 - 1880 | U.S. History Primary Source Timeline | Classroom Materials at the Library of Congress | Library of Congress" *Library of Congress*, 1 Mar. 2021, www.loc.gov/classroom-materials/united-states-history-primary-source-timeline/national-expansion-and-reform-1815-1880/pre-civil-war-african-american-slavery/.

Lewan, Todd. "Landownership made blacks targets of violence and murder" *The Authentic Voice*, theauthenticvoice.org/mainstories/tornfromtheland/torn_part2/.

Hasso, Jennifer. "The Green Book" *Jim Crow Museum, Ferris State University*, 2021, www.ferris.edu/HTMLS/news/jimcrow/question/2021/september.htm.

"Section 51, Song of Myself" *IWP WhitmanWeb*, iwp.uiowa.edu/whitmanweb/en/writings/song-of-myself/section-51.

Lesson Five

"History of Rawlins" https://www.rawlinswy.gov/191/History-of-Rawlins

Creamer, Colleen. "In 5 National Parks, Hidden Gems and Roads Less Traveled" *New York Times*, 20 July 2022, https://www.nytimes.com/2022/07/20/travel/national-parks-hidden-gems.html.

Elkhorn Ranch Unit, Teddy Roosevelt National Park, North Dakota, "Visit the Elkhorn Ranch Unit" *U.S. National Park Service*, www.nps.gov/thingstodo/visit-the-elkhorn-ranch-unit.htm.

"To Be Is To Do To Do Is To Be Do Be Do Be Do" *Quote Investigator*, 16 Sept. 2013, quoteinvestigator.com/2013/09/16/do-be-do/.

Kurtz, Ernest and Katherine Ketcham. "The Spirituality of Imperfection" *Penguin Random House*, 1 Dec 1993, www.penguinrandomhouse.com/books/96307/the-spirituality-of-imperfection-by-ernest-kurtz-and-katherine-ketcham/.

Luke 2:25-35, New Revised Standard Version (NRSV)

Stephens, Dustin. "The debate over the Geographical Center of North America" *CBS News*, 30 May 2021, www.cbsnews.com/news/the-geographical-center-of-north-america/.

The Labyrinth Society, https://labyrinthsociety.org/

Lesson Six

Rest Area History, https://restareahistory.org/.

Keillor, Garrison. "The Tollefson Boy Goes to College." *Prairie Home Companion*, www.youtube.com/watch?v=FRT8YlMWmgM.

Little America, Wyoming, https://wyoming.littleamerica.com/.

"Lincoln Highway-Little America" *Wyoming Tales and Trails*, www.wyomingtalesandtrails.com/littleamerica.html.

The Historic Dyess Colony: Johnny Cash Boyhood Home, Dyess, Arkansas, https://dyesscash.astate.edu/

Elvis Presley Birthplace, Tupelo, Mississippi, https://elvispresleybirthplace.com/

Guitar Walk, Walnut Ridge, Arkansas, https://www.beatlesattheridge.com/attractions/guitar-walk/

Beatles Park, Walnut Ridge, Arkansas, https://www.beatlesattheridge.com/attractions/beatles-park/

Ozark Folk Center, Mountain View, Arkansas, https://www.arkansasstateparks.com/parks/ozark-folk-center-state-park

Metropolis, Illinois, https://www.metropolistourism.com/

Mackinaw Pastie, Mackinaw City, Michigan, https://www.mackinawpastie.com/

"WRVK's "Living Legend" Pete Stamper!" *WRVK 1460*, www.wrvk1460.com/pete-stamper.HTM.

Blankenship, Jessica. "Life of country music comedian Pete Stamper celebrated" *Kentucky Country Music*, 26 July 2020, kentuckycountrymusic.com/2020/07/pete-stamper-memorial.html.

Lesson Seven

Herdsman House in Neubergthal, Manitoba, https://www.airbnb.com/rooms/22516534

"What's a Schlafenbank/Schlopbenkj? A Sleeping Bench!" Mennonite Heritage and Agricultural Museum Facebook Page, 19 May 2022, https://www.facebook.com/MennoniteHeritageandAgriculturalMuseum/photos/a.271797289924892/1457773144660628/?type=3

Neubergthal Heritage Foundation, Village History, https://www.neubergthalheritagefoundation.com/village-history, Hausbarns: https://www.neubergthalheritagefoundation.com/friesen-housebarn

"Neubergthal Story: Russian stove rebuilt" *Masonry Heater Association of North America*, https://www.mha-net.org/docs/v8n2/docs/Neubergthal-Story.pdf

"Anishinaabe" *The Canadian Encyclopedia*, www.thecanadianencyclopedia.ca/en/article/anishinaabe.

Scandinavian Heritage Park and Association, Minot, ND https://scandinavianheritage.org/

Prairie Outpost Park, Dickinson Museum Center, Dickinson, ND, https://dickinsonmuseumcenter.com/prairie-outpost-park/

"Fourth Thursday in History: Calumet's Catholic Churches" *Keweenaw National Historical Park*, www.nps.gov/kewe/learn/news/calumet-catholic-churches.htm.

"List of Federal and State Recognized Tribes" *www.ncsl.org/legislators-staff/legislators/quad-caucus/list-of-federal-and-state-recognized-tribes.aspx.*

Matthew 2:16–18, NRSV

Jeremiah 52:10–11, NRSV

Exodus 1:22, NRSV

International Peace Garden, Boissevain, Manitoba, https://peacegarden.com/.

International Peace Gardens, Jordan Park, Salt Lake City, Utah, https://www.internationalpeacegardens.org/.

Lesson Eight

Bay View Association, Bay View, Michigan, https://www.bayviewassociation.org/.

"The Chautauqua Trail" *A North American Cultural Renaissance*, www.chautauqua-trail.com.

Rousmaniere, Peter. "A mosque in Nebraska" *Working Immigrants*, 22 Jan. 2019, www.workingimmigrants.com/2019/01/a-mosque-in-nebraska/.

Ikerd, John. "The Economic Colonization of Rural America" *The Daily Yonder*, 28 Feb. 2018, dailyyonder.com/economic-colonization-rural-america/2018/02/28/.

Benfield, Kaid. "How to retrofit failing suburban big box stores into a green showcase" 12 March 2012, Kaid Benfield Archive, https://kaidbenfieldarchive.com/20120312-how-to-retrofit-failing-suburban-big-box-stores-into-a.html.

Benfield, Kaid. "What Does a 'Sustainable Community' Actually Look Like?" *The Atlantic*, 14 Mar. 2011, www.theatlantic.com/national/archive/2011/03/what-does-a-sustainable-community-actually-look-like/72376/.

Putnam, Robert D. *Bowling Alone: The Collapse and Revival of American Community*. New York: Simon & Schuster, 2020.

Bellah, Robert N. *Habits of the Heart: Individualism and Commitment in American Life*. New York: Harper & Row, 1986

Brach, Tara. *Radical Acceptance: Embracing Your Life With the Heart of a Buddha*, New York, Random House, 2004.

Lesson Nine

Clements, J. B. *History of Irwin County*. 1932. http://files.usgwarchives.net/ga/irwin/history/other/gms27historyo.txt

"Old Coffee Road, Georgia" *WWALS Watershed Coalition*, 3 Sept. 2017, wwals.net/2017/09/03/old-coffee-road-georgia/.

"Noted Indian Settlement" *Historical Marker Database*, https://www.hmdb.org/m.asp?m=9844

Ambler's Texaco Gas Station, Dwight, Illinois, https://www.nps.gov/nr/travel/route66/amblers_texaco_gasstation_dwight.html

Mother Jones Monument, Mt. Olive, Illinois, https://www.motherjonesmuseum.org/motherjonesmonument

Ariston Cafe, Litchfield, Illinois, https://www.ariston-cafe.com/.

Litchfield Museum and Route 66 Welcome Center, Litchfield, Illinois, http://www.litchfieldmuseum.org/.

"Elvis Presley's Childhood Church, Tupelo, Mississippi" *Historical Marker Database*, https://www.hmdb.org/m.asp?m=29821.

The Great Passion Play, Eureka Springs, Arkansas, https://www.greatpassionplay.org/.

The Creation History Museum at the Great Passion Play, Eureka Springs, Arkansas, http://nwabiblemuseum.org/.

The Sacred Arts Center at the Great Passion Play, Eureka Springs, Arkansas, https://www.greatpassionplay.org/sacred-arts-museum.html.

The Bible Museum at the Great Passion Play, Eureka Springs, Arkansas, https://www.greatpassionplay.org/bible-museum.html.

Thorncrown Chapel, https://thorncrown.com/.

DuTemple, Lesley. "Our Snowshoe Saint" *Lake Superior Magazine*, 30 July 2018, www.lakesuperior.com/travel/michigan/402snowshoe-saint-the-long-trek-to-sainthood-for-father-frederi/.

Utah Pride Center, https://utahpridecenter.org/.

> For more on how learning can transform us, check out my book Life After: Finding Strength and Spirit in Unexpected Change, at https://www.canemillpress.com/home/life-after.

www.ingramcontent.com/pod-product-compliance
Lightning Source LLC
Chambersburg PA
CBHW050028130526
44590CB00042B/2046